Client Perceptions of Being in Therapy

And how they relate to client problems

For Therapists and Curious Clients

Mamood Ahmad

© 2020

Also by the same Author:

Success in Therapy

Subscribe to **Dear Therapist (on YouTube)**
for weekly videos about mental health and therapy

Twitter: @ahmad_mamood

Client Perception of Being in Therapy

Published by PT Publishing (Bracknell, UK)

PathTherapy, St. Marks Road, Bracknell, RG42 4AN, UK

Empoweringyourtherapy.com

First Edition

ISBN: 9798638407360

Contents

Introduction

This book aims to explore the ways in which clients perceive therapy and thus themselves, regardless of their unique circumstances and problem(s), during the therapeutic process. These perceptions include how they ought to conduct themselves in therapy, their relationship with the therapist and their difficulties in navigating the therapeutic process.

The premise of this exploration is the widely accepted belief that therapy can be conceived as a miniature version (or microcosm) of the client's real world, and however clients operate in their world—which includes their beliefs, emotions and behaviours—they can surface in the therapeutic process.

Traditionally, this microcosm has focused in on the therapeutic relationship. However, this book extends that exploration to include the way clients use therapy, and their beliefs about how they should conduct themselves in therapy. These beliefs about how they "should" be, their feelings about the therapist, and their difficulties during therapy could reveal much about the client's inner world, and importantly how these perceptions relate to their problems.

So, let's look at a couple of examples from a client's perspective, and discover how awareness of the client's process within the construct of therapy can come about in the room

In the pattern of "I'm a good client", you may be unaware that you are wanting to perform and to please the therapist, but as you work more in therapy, you come to recognise the "mask" of being a good client has more to do with feeling scared of "getting things wrong". So becoming aware of the process of being a "good client" can get you more in touch with what's going on and so work with these feelings in the room.

In another pattern, "relational cracks", you are consciously aware of feeling irritated with the therapist. You put it in the back of your mind, but it inadvertently infects the process and blocks you from feeling comfortable around the relationship and from being more vulnerable. You are not fully aware that this is hurting your process. The therapist is also unaware of your irritation at his suggestions. Eventually, therapy ends because it's not going anywhere. The chance to repair the foundation of therapy is lost.

In the process of "Am I crazy?" Louis expresses himself over the course of 10 minutes about his feelings towards his work colleagues. The therapist notices a pause where Louis changes the subject and starts talking about decorations on the wall. Something similar happened in the previous session. The therapist asks "I noticed there was a pause and a shift between your feelings. I wondered what happened for you?" Louis explains that he felt uneasy when talking for that long, and that the therapist must have been thinking he was crazy. Here the client was aware of his process so he stopped talking, but through the therapist's curiosity his process was made available to explore in the room.

In the process "careful" you become aware that when you express your thoughts—particularly about your personal life—you rehearse what you say to the therapist in your mind first. You catch this process and tell the therapist.

This book is written for both therapists and curious clients. For therapists, trainee therapists and tutors, this book illuminates an important layer of process information that could easily be overlooked, yet is of therapeutic value. It can be used as a source of reflection both in the classroom and in practice. For clients, this book can be used as a general learning resource to help you get the most from your experience. If something resonates, I suggest spending time on it and, if appropriate, follow it through into therapy.

What this book covers

This book contains over 40 themes which clients could surface in relation to therapy, outside of their own unique circumstances and history. For structure I have divided these themes into the following chapters:

- Chapter 1 – Themes of therapeutic effectiveness. Process patterns that relate to usage of the instrument of therapy.
- Chapter 2 – Themes of the therapeutic relationship. Process patterns that relate to your relationship with the therapist.
- Chapter 3 – Themes of surfacing beliefs. Process patterns that relate to beliefs you have about therapy and thus potentially about yourself.
- Chapter 4 - To understand a bit more about the theory of change in therapy, what changes, and a model of how the process unfolds.
- Appendix A – Further Support for Consumers in Therapy

Who is this book for?

If you are a therapist, therapist trainer, supervisor or trainee therapist, you could utilise this resource for your own study, for continuous professional development, or to review how you introduce process-related themes to clients. Of course, providing this as reading material for clients may be appropriate too.

This books is also for the curious consumer and for anyone interested in, considering or beginning their therapeutic process.

Important points

When reading and understanding the material in this book please bear the following in mind:

- In order for the themes to be accessible to clients I address clients directly.

- The intention is to empower your therapy process and strengthen the work you are doing, not interfere with it. If you feel safe, consult the therapist about strategies and decisions you make as a result of reading this book.

- This book is based on generic therapy processes and is neutral to any type (or modality) of therapy or problem. It has been reviewed by a number of UK qualified therapists across the spectrum: psychodynamic, person-centred, existential, integrative and CBT. This does not mean that all therapists will agree completely with all the material presented. Therefore, it is highly recommended you talk about things that come from this book with your therapist.

- The book assumes you are working with a "good-enough" therapist —one who can accept all your feelings and work with them, with empathy and acceptance. They can make occasional mistakes but overall, you feel safe with them. Therapists may give their perspective, even counter to yours, but they do so with your interests in mind. However, just like all professions, there is no guarantee how well informed or sensitive your therapist is.

Chapter 1 – Themes of therapeutic effectiveness

The themes in this chapter relate to potential difficulties with the efficient and effective use of therapy (as opposed to the content of the work you're doing).

Maybe you want the therapist to "guide you", your therapy is "hitting a wall", or you've become overly "dependent" on therapy. As with all the themes in this book, not all will be applicable to you, but if any resonate, then that is a good opportunity for further self-reflection and potential work with the therapist. Of course, that does not mean there is a deeper meaning in your process, as it could be just a learning point that needs to be clarified by the therapist during the process.

See Chapter 3 for themes which relate to the therapeutic relationship.

No time to heal

When there is a physical injury, our body tells us very quickly when something is wrong. If we injure our leg, we are soon aware of our condition because of pain or a limitation, such as not being able to move the leg freely. We usually realise because of these symptoms and their impact on us that we need to seek help. A doctor may suggest we go on some medication, do some exercises, and go through a rehabilitation programme of physiotherapy and rest to take off the full weight of the body on the leg. We may have to take a bit of time off work, forgo the exercise we once enjoyed and reduce our social activity. If we do not heed the advice of doctors and give ourselves time to heal, we could end up in a cycle of recovery that is far longer, and our leg may get worse, causing a more permanent impact. Bottom line: if we don't give time or priority to the injury, we don't give ourselves the best chance to recover.

In comparison with mental health, it is common to ignore psychological symptoms because of their lack of externally visible signs. With psychological symptoms, such as anxiety or prolonged low moods, we can still be highly functioning and have no apparent physical limitations, so we may choose to ignore them and carry on business as usual. Even when we know something is wrong, we may end up putting it off and even feel ashamed of the stigma of seeking mental health support. We may make some moves to help ourselves, like get more sleep, but we don't fully perform the necessary steps to give us the best chance of recovery. For example, we may continue working long hours and continue to expose ourselves to mentally stressful situations, causing our anxiety to spiral. A voice may be saying something is wrong but because we appear to be functioning "as-if" these problems were non-existent, the symptoms become easier to ignore. The necessary care is simply not present. After a while, our mental health issues can start interfering not just "inside" of our mind but they can also spill over into the physical symptoms and impact external situations, such as anxiety at work, panic attacks and not being able to enjoy life anymore. Just like walking on an injured leg, the more we "push through" emotional injuries, the more the issues can grow and the emotional injury gets bigger and more severe, increasing the time we need to recover fully. It could even result in what is popularly referred to as a "nervous breakdown" where the level of depression, anxiety or dissociation is to such an extent that you are not able to function without resolution.

Mental health requires metaphorically the same type of attitude to healing as a physical injury. This may include finding time to heal, changing lifestyle, and seeking support, advice and therapy. Therefore, the commitment to the act of a therapeutic process is analogous to not simply pushing through and standing on an injured leg but giving yourself the "space" mentally to work on yourself. By working on recovery through therapy, you are accepting the fact that there is an emotional injury, just as you would for a physical injury. Through accepting the need to make changes to recover, we are doing the equivalent of taking the weight off our emotional injury, which provides us a clear space to heal emotionally.

If you feel this is you, perhaps it's time to explore that further because sometimes, people are good at valuing others more, or they are less inclined to treat themselves as well.

Self-Reflection

1. Do you suffer from any psychological problem, e.g., low moods, anxiety, stress, fears or sadness?
2. How are you generally with caring about yourself? Attending to yourself and your needs?
3. Do you give yourself time and priority when it comes to your wellbeing? If not, why?
4. As an experiment, think about someone you have responsibility for or care deeply about. It could be a child or an elderly parent. Now, imagine they are struggling with the same problems you are experiencing. What advice and/or care would you provide them? Would your approach to care change? Would the priorities change? Would you invest time and money on them?
5. If you believe you need to spend more time on yourself, how can you achieve that? For example, you could change priorities or give yourself more time and space in your spare time.

I know

Socrates, the Greek philosopher, was astonished when the oracle of Delphi said, "There is no one wiser than Socrates!" He did not believe that of himself, and asked, how could that be? Given the reliability of the source, he spent time investigating various experts on all matters to determine how that could be. He finally came to a conclusion and said, "Ah, I get it: they think they know something, but I know I know absolutely nothing."

That's part of how therapy can be effective: be tentative about what you know about yourself, what will be the solution and what will happen next. Be fluid and open to the idea you don't know everything yet and any conclusions are tentative as you go through your journey. For example, do you know what is causing the symptoms? do you know what you understand about yourself and your needs, and your childhood?

Why is this important? Well, it is a bit like excavating an archaeological site for treasures and thinking there are no more rooms left to explore after two or three, when there may be dozens more; you don't know, but you reserve that judgement. Your awareness and understanding of yourself and how that influences your issues is usually of paramount importance when healing. Blocking further investigation can pre-emptively block access to more inner doors. Simply put, any understanding you have may not be the whole picture.

A classic way of describing this need for tentative knowledge we have was laid out by Sigmund Freud. He describes what we know about ourselves as an iceberg: the tip of the iceberg is what we know about, yet there is a whole lot more going on underneath!

A narrative that may indicate a block to further discoveries may sound something like this:

"[beginning therapy] I've been through therapy before over many years. So I know it's about my anger towards my parents. I don't think repeating that with you is going to make a difference. I've also done the 'punch the bag' and 'get your anger out' bit. Can you give me some techniques to make this anxiety drop?"

Other types of voices that may indicate this type of thinking include "there is nothing that can be done now,", "I don't see how this can help,", "I know that already," or "I had a good childhood." While these feelings are real and are to be respected; having an open mind to other possibilities and new experiences can open up new possibilities, particularly if the problems still remain.

Here is a narrative of what happens when you discover something new about yourself in therapy:

"I never knew my work-performance anxiety was also to do with how I felt that my mum took sides with my stepfather rather than with me. I thought this was really all about my boss at work. I don't know how, but exploring that stuff seemed to help with my anxiety at work. I poured my heart out to my mum, and hearing her say sorry helped."

Note: confronting people about harm they caused you is always something I recommend reflecting on in therapy first.

During therapy, be open and curious about yourself, people and the world around you. Learn about yourself just like you would go about any type of learning. For example, if as you learn to juggle balls, you accept that it's a process, you'll learn by experience and making mistakes, and in your own time, you will improve. You can only know what you know about how to juggle at a point in time even with assistance. You only know what you know at a point in time; there is plenty more to learn, and that applies to yourself too.

Have no conclusions, don't assume where things will lead to and what can or will help the most. Letting go of fixed conclusions leaves the door open for new ideas, possibilities and ultimately growth and healing. You don't assume you know the answers until of course you're in a better place or at the end of therapy. It is common for life-long travellers to never say they have seen all parts of the world, and that can apply to yourself too. Socrates believed he knew nothing, and that is the true spirit of living and learning.

Self-Reflection

1. How do you generally approach learning, e.g., a hobby, learning to use a device or even some DIY project?
2. Do you learn analytically by following instructions or by feel and through experience?
3. Do you notice what you feel during the process of learning? Feelings including being absorbed, frustration, impatience, or wanting the learning process to end or continue further.
4. How do you feel usually when someone else knows more about a subject than you? How does it feel in competitive situations? School? And at home?
5. Do you feel you are open to learning and letting the therapist help you?

I can fix it

Fred came to counselling because of the relationship difficulties he was having with his wife. He had a turbulent history with his stepson, and he often clashed with his wife over him. It had gotten to a stage where he was feeling disconnected with his wife and things were not being shared freely between them. It felt like he was in a triangle, and she would keep the relationship with her son away from him. Fred shared their history, the pains and how his stepson had disrespected him many times. He understood what he was feeling, and at the end, he decided to reach out to his stepson to try and fix it. But as a few sessions proceeded, he could not understand why he was not feeling any better and neither was she. They continued to be short with one another, distant and missing each other's needs. What was going on? What was missing?

It was only when he got in touch with his true feelings –feelings of being second-best and anger that his wife would allow her son to get away with things, even though she knew her son could be very "difficult." He realised why his fix of reaching out to his stepson and talking to his wife was a start and not a fix. So although reconciliation with his stepson was welcomed by his wife, it hid the anger, resentment and pain that was buried deep within him. His anger of being left out, her anger at him, and their 18-year history of turbulence, so no matter his reconciliation with her son, it could not fix his relationship with her.

Fred and his wife took up the suggestion of couples counselling and engaged in a process over a number of months to heal their real underlying feelings of resentment, disappointment and hurt. Fred and his wife realised that fixing things was only a start, and that a natural inclination towards a quick-fix was not possible because of missed or dormant feelings. They learnt that through experience, the answer lay not in the apparent fix, but in the process of healing, which includes reciprocal understanding of feelings, and understanding what happened and why. Only then did the underlying feelings begin to subside and move on. The fix was not the answer; the process was the answer.

In another example, the process can be missed because of assumptions about what would make healing work:

Jim came to therapy looking for answers. He would often analyse his feelings, thoughts and childhood. He wanted answers in the hope that by having the answer, he would be able to relieve himself of symptoms of feeling low. He was quick to be anxious and frustrated in session that he could not find it. Later, he discovered there were many reasons for this but one factor was his assumption that he had to find the golden answer. But in fact, by processing his feelings in the here and now, and by simply being with his feelings, somehow over time, he began to feel better. He had assumed nothing would happen unless he found something, an analytical answer, when in fact, his commitment to the process, including time and effort, allowed him to heal. He had assumed that since nothing was being found out in therapy, nothing was happening in his recovery. What was happening underneath was that he let go of thinking there was a single golden egg to be found in the basket of recovery.

If you are not getting anywhere with trying to fix a problem, consider whether that fix bypasses the process. The process is a continuous journey, full of ideas, insights, feelings and new perceptions. The journey of healing usually requires a process rather than a fix.

Self-Reflection

1. When something goes wrong, what do you normally try to do in life? How do you handle it? Think about the answer for emotionally distressing situations, e.g., stress, grief as well as practical matters, such as finances or a complaint.
2. How do you demonstrate your way of caring when someone is going through a difficult time, such as stress, difficult life events, and bereavement? (Ideas: avoid, fix it by direct suggestions, listening, empathy, understanding, hugs)
3. Ask yourself and someone else what they need when things out of their control go wrong or when they make a mistake?

Guide me

Therapy is all about empowering you to create your own understanding, make decisions, to gain access to feelings and to be able to relate them. The therapist is there to help you focus inside yourself in order to change. They won't tell you what to do or provide a specific answer to "what, how and why." If you are looking for guidance in the traditional sense, it is easy to see why it could be frustrating to be in therapy, as the therapist does not "guide" you. Most of the time, they won't set the agenda, tell you what is going on with you, or what you need to do; rather, they will stay within your understanding, reflect back, see and feel. Although some types of therapy can offer more interpretations of what is going on for you, they in general help you find the answers within which only you could possibly answer and decide upon.

Expressing what's going on in your heart, mind, and body is really important in therapy. Only through your expression can both you and your therapist experience and understand your world. Although therapists may talk more at the beginning to help you open up, eventually you'll need to learn to do most of the talking yourself. Therapy is a collaboration, but in the long run it's you taking the therapist on a journey inside your experiences, not the other way around.

Of course, therapists do express themselves from their perspective too; they can express feelings, ask questions, structure sessions, set the agenda, offer feedback, or suggest what may be going on for you. Expressing yourself does not mean you do not use the therapist. If you are stuck, need feedback, or have questions, you should feel free to ask. By sharing what you need you are expressing yourself from your point of view.

Here is a narrative to demonstrate how therapy can differ from the guidance we may naturally expect from other types of experts or even friends:

Peter felt he wanted answers and ideas of how the current and past events relate. He had been feeling in the dark and wanted to know where to begin. The therapist didn't tell him exactly what was expected and instead chose to offer a feeling.

Peter: How do I make sense of what is going on? My feelings? To the past?

Therapist: I can hear you really struggle when you are looking for an answer. I would like to help you find it. What comes up?

Client: But that is not guidance surely? It does not tell me anything really.

Therapist: When you previously tried to "join the dots," you asked me and eventually you found something, even though it wasn't easy. How does that work for you?

If this resonates this can then lead into a whole new door of exploration. For example, what did Peter's lack of self-trust in being his own guide mean? In therapy, direct guidance is rarely given. However, the guidance comes in a different form, the form that focuses on you finding your own truth. Turning the light on inside you is the equivalent of guidance, but therapeutic guidance.

Wanting the therapist to guide you

When Fran began to express herself, I noticed she would say a few words and then pause, look at me and wait. I wondered what Fran was expressing to me when she did that.

If you catch yourself wanting to use the therapist's perspective a lot or wanting to stay away from your own, then you can be curious about the nature of your experience. You can use it as a source for exploration.

Here are some possible reasons to explore:

- You need guidance on what to do.
- You believe that's the way therapy should be done.
- You want the therapist to focus the agenda or structure.
- You don't feel safe yet. For example, you feel judged or don't trust your therapist.
- You don't want to say the wrong things and so need for them to reassure you.
- It's too difficult for you to stay within your own experience and just express whatever is going on.
- It's a way of life. For example, you're not used to taking "air space" or having people listen to you.

Whatever your need for staying outside of your own point of view, it is an opportunity to explore it in therapy. It may even relate very much to the problem you are working on.

Self-Reflection

1. Who are the people in life that tended to guide you? When was it helpful? Or detrimental?
2. Do you find it easy to make decisions?
3. Do you struggle to make decisions or find answers in home, family, social circles or in therapy?
4. Who do you go to for guidance?
5. Do you think the guidance is always good, forthcoming or available?
6. Do you think the answers are relevant to your problems you are trying to overcome in therapy?

Locked up

What if opening up is too difficult? Therapists recognise that opening up for some can be the hardest part of therapy and they have no preconceived expectations of how you "should" be in therapy, whether you find expressing yourself difficult or are not ready to. They will work with you "as you are" with empathy and without judgement. They take time and will not criticise or blame you for whatever you experience. They are there to help you.

Clients who are initially anxious about opening up quite often find their worries or anxieties diminish considerably once their feelings and experiences are validated and normalised. Sharing difficulties opening up can take the sting out of the encounter.

Difficulties with opening up can of course be very much related to the problem you're trying to overcome, as it was for Fran.

Fran always kept herself to herself. In school, girls would often shame her in front of the whole class, laughing and pointing at her: "Err, look at her, she's weird, what's wrong with her, why doesn't she say anything!" Fran would put her head down, looking towards the floor so she could escape. She didn't want anyone to see her upset. Instead, her anger would come out towards herself while alone, going from anger to tears. Years later, the tears dried out and she spoke little about herself. Fran entered therapy as an adult wanting help to stop fearing social situations.

Fran felt really awkward in therapy. Her mind was rushing, trying to find things to say. Often she would get upset or angry with herself in front of the therapist because she could not open up. She found therapy so hard because of her difficulties in expressing herself in front of a stranger; it felt like so much pressure she would often go home with a migraine.

For Fran, the therapy encounter was emotionally triggering, at least in part due to her social anxiety. Often, difficulties opening up relate to your experiences and the problems you're trying to overcome. If you recognise that your difficulties with opening up are related to your problems, it can be a useful way of reinterpreting your therapy, because instead of seeing opening up as an obstacle to begin therapy, it can be seen as being a central theme to your therapy. Developing awareness of your underlying feelings about opening up can provide you and your therapist important areas to explore. For example, feeling that you're going to be judged, or you won't be able to manage emotions, or feeling embarrassed are all worth exploring.

Of course this is not the only reason why opening up could be difficult. For example, worries about personal ability, consequences of change, or whether the therapist will understand you.

Regardless of why you are having difficulties, here are some self-help strategies for you. As everyone is unique, you will need to assess for yourself which of these strategies would help.

Be safe
If the encounter is too distressing, then tell the therapist or even stop the session. You don't want to hurt yourself emotionally by pushing through when you are clearly distressed. Consult your therapist and doctor.

Use the therapist
Remember, therapists are very familiar with difficulties in opening up and are experts in guiding you through the process. If you are already in therapy, you can explore the difficulty of opening up with the therapist. Although the therapist is likely to guide you, here are three strategies you can ask for:

- You can reflect on what you need from the therapist to help you open up; for example, maybe all you need is space and time, rather than being under pressure to talk.
- Ask the therapist to see if they can ask you questions that you can answer, rather than having to come up with things to say.
- You can also ask the therapist if they can do something with you that isn't directly face to face. For example, use emotion cards or an expressive art (remember, art is not about being a good artist!). Another example, is to use a notepad and pen to communicate.

By taking the step to express your difficulties and needs, you're already on your way to opening up.

Evaluate expectations
Clients can often put so much pressure on themselves to "perform" or be a "good client" that it can get in the way of opening up. If you recognise this in you, then that is likely to have therapeutic value, so it's worth telling your therapist about. Remember, therapy is about focusing in on you and your goals rather than coming up with things to say to fill silence or please the therapist. So even if you're silent, which I know can be awkward at first, you can learn to become more comfortable with it.

Dear Diary
You can consider using a diary to write about the topics you want to express, including difficulties you are having expressing yourself. Write a few points down and bring it into a session as a point of reference, or even send it in securely prior to your session. Expressing yourself in writing can be a good way to learn to develop confidence in opening up.

Consider other sources of expression

Consider whether there are other sources you can draw upon to gradually open up. For example, expressing how you would like to be in the future. If you find it easier to talk about certain subjects, then that is the important first step.

Many clients forget that what they experience in the here and now can be a useful source of expression. This is where you take a step back to notice your feelings, body sensations, and thoughts and verbalise them with the therapist. For example: My heart is running fast, I feel awkward, or I feel like escaping.

Consider online therapy

Consider whether another medium, such as phone calls, outdoor therapy, or instant messaging approaches, would make opening up easier. Many online therapists are able to move from instant messaging, to phone, to face to face therapy as and when you are ready.

Let things brew

If you're not ready to open up because you don't feel quite safe yet, then you can wait until you're ready. Like in most relationships, building trust can take time and although it's difficult now, that does not mean it won't change over time. You don't need to feel you owe the therapist trust, it's a process like in every relationship.

Consider ending therapy

Alternatively, if you believe it's not working because of the particular therapist you're seeing, you can consider ending the relationship with that therapist.

Remember, however you express yourself, the therapist will work you as you are, with empathy and without judgement.

What if disclosure is too difficult?

And then there was the subject of what Fran really wanted help with. Being raped by her mother's boyfriend. She was frozen then and she is frozen now.

For Fran, disclosure of her rape in therapy is a scary experience and the range of underlying feelings that make it scary is something that will most certainly need exploring in therapy. However, her reasons for holding back are likely to fall into one of more of the following areas:

- You're just not ready to talk about a particular problem or experience.
- The disclosure is loaded with feelings about being judged and you feel it's something shameful or embarrassing.
- You're worried that you or someone you know will get into trouble because of the disclosure. For example, in the case of a criminal act that someone you know has committed.

- You think what you share would be used against you, whether by an insurer, employer, court, or government.
- You don't want personal information to be stored or shared. For example, in therapists' records or to friends and family.
- Some other unique reason. For example, you don't want to disclose because the person won't be in your life when therapy ends.

As it happens, Fran was not so concerned about telling the therapist. What she was more worried about was her mother abandoning her because the therapist reported it. For Fran, disclosure did not feel like an option.

Given the dilemmas clients face and the possible repercussions, it's not surprising if you feel some reluctance to disclose. Most often in my experience, a client's worries about repercussions are usually unfounded, but it depends on the context. If it's a worry, then you can use the following self-help strategies to help you towards feeling safer about disclosure.

Find out the facts
Many clients can be worried about what the therapist will do with information they disclose and whether it will harm them in some way. If you are worried about the confidentiality of what you disclose, you could open up a dialogue by asking what the limits of confidentiality are. Often therapists and organisations have a written disclosure policy.

Use the therapist
If you're finding it difficult to disclose something important for your therapy, you can start by exploring your worries about disclosure rather than disclosing. Through that process, you'll be exploring your feelings of reluctance and in doing so may feel more comfortable to disclose.

Use a content free approach
Many therapists work with you in a "content free" way, so you don't have to disclose. Using a content free approach, the therapist directs you into your experience and you talk about feelings and sensations rather than disclosing what happened. Some therapies, such as EMDR, EFT, Focusing Therapy or NLP, contain *"content free"* protocols within them. Other approaches may include the use of metaphor, art, and sand trays to help you through your feelings.

Talk to your therapist to see whether they can work this way and whether it could be beneficial given the context of your goals.

Other strategies include:

- Online therapy, particularly where the service is provided anonymously. Anonymous services can still have limits of confidentiality.
- Consider writing a letter to read out loud or securely send to the therapist
- Consider whether you can allow yourself more time before disclosure. Maybe you aren't quite ready to disclose but you're working towards it.
- Consider whether you feel safe enough with the therapist and whether you need to end therapy.

Ultimately, you are free to choose whether you disclose or not; you can wait or decide at a later date. If the disclosure is important to your process, then you will have to look at whether it's something you can realistically work on without exploring.

Knowing what to bring up

Sometimes particularly if your analytical minded you may wonder what it is that you need to focus on to get the most out of therapy. This can itself cause confusion and frustration regardless of whether you are working towards specific goals or are working in an open ended manner. This is not something that can be answered in absolute terms because it depends on your circumstances. But it is an understandable particularly if your mind is overloaded with possibilities or you have a set number of sessions to work with.

However, experience and theory indicates that the mind finds its own way once it begin expressing yourself. So what may seem irrelevant or way off mark can branch off into very important therapeutic material over time. In practice this means "trusting" your mind to eventually know what's important to bring up.

Here are some more ideas to reflect on in therapy:

- You can accept that you don't know
- What pops up in the here and now is usually a good start to expression
- What you push away as difficult when determining what you need to talk can often be something to talk about
- Ask whether what you are talking about relates to your goals
- Does "not knowing" relate to your difficulties? For example, control, perfection or wanting to get it right.
- Tell the therapist and let them guide you in their own way

This type of worry can occur when you're in a hurry or may be related to your problem too. This is something of course to talk to your therapist about.

Self-Reflection

1. How comfortable are you with talking about your thoughts, feelings and perspectives?
2. How much do you usually share about yourself with friends, family, colleagues, and strangers? Do you listen more or talk more?
3. How do you feel about the prospect of sharing with a therapist, even things you have never shared with anyone before?
4. What, if anything, in this way applies to you?
5. If you have trouble expressing parts of yourself, reflect on why that is.
6. What do you need from the therapist to be able to freely share what you need to?

Dipping toes

We've all done it, spending time wondering or thinking about what it would be like to achieve a desired goal, whether it's getting a dream job, building that house extension or swimming better. But we all know that eventually, we're going to have to put those ideas into a plan of action and actually go through the process of achieving that goal – training, choosing materials or applying for jobs. To get better at swimming, we may seek guidance from a teacher, but we know that it's only through regular experience of swimming where improvements lie – it simply is not much help to only dip our toes in the water when we want to improve our front stroke.

A narrative of someone who focuses a lot on the outcome and goal may sound like this:

"I really wish I could get better. I can't believe I'm like this. I really don't know why I am; I just want to get better. I just feel life is passing by. I don't know if I ever will be able to get better. I can feel panicky and anxious. I just want to feel better so I can meet someone, get married one day and enjoy my life, but instead, I have to spend time and money coming to therapy. I don't know what to do. Tell me what I need to do."

This expresses a natural sentiment of someone wanting to improve to achieve life goals. However, when this narrative occupies a large amount of therapy time, the worry of achieving goals and what you ought to be like needs to be checked so it does not dominate the experience and process of therapy.

Rather, focus on the experience of therapy by focusing on lived-in life experiences, memories, stresses and feelings rather than just the issues, symptoms and goals. Someone engaged in the process can sound a bit like this:

"I do feel panicky in groups. It all started a couple years ago. I was out with my friends and I went to the bathroom. I returned and all my friends had moved to a different table just like a prank. But when I came back, I felt really angry and shouted at everyone, and I thought it was really mean. The feelings were overwhelming and confusing at the same time."

Similarly, the active process of therapy can be halted if there is a lot of emphasis on day-to-day activity, interpretation or analysing yourself, sometimes referred to as "analysis paralysis." This can also be very useful "grist in the mill," but when they dominate most of the time in the room, they can keep you from experiencing therapy.

A contrast between analysis and experience may sound something like this:

"Over the weekend, I felt no one was talking to me, and I know why. I know it goes back to my childhood because I was bullied. I just need to accept that."

A more experiential statement may be:

"The feeling I had over the weekend was as if I was back at school with people laughing at me or ignoring me. I felt so alone.. angry. I went home and thought, what is the point of me trying anymore?"

In the first example, you are making an assessment but are removed from the experience, as if it was happening to someone else. The second statement uses language indicating a more lived-in experience, a first person or "I" experience rather than distant, as if it is removed from you.

Another way of limiting the experience of therapy is by focusing a lot of time on the reason for a problem or issue as if that alone will "cure" you of your problems. Focusing on awareness and contribution of events is important, but it can be like a dead-end to say, "Only if I knew the answer to why this happened." Of course that will be relevant, but therapy is an experience too; it's about allowing your mind to go where it naturally wants, such as in lived-in memories, association of ideas, joining the dots, awareness, felt responses, grief, re-perception, mental insights and subtle shifts. Just knowing the answer may not be enough to resolve things, but it can open doors; therefore, the reasons can in many cases be treated as a means to an end rather than an end.

Similarly, you may feel that the answer lies in something in the past, which is understandable, such as in a trauma or physical abuse. You say, "If only I could remember." Remembering would be really useful, but if you can't, you may be able to later. Remembering, in general, is not mandatory for healing. For example, not being able to locate exactly when you first dissociated does not mean the process has to end. Here and now feelings and thoughts in the body can be healed without necessarily knowing the full content of the past

Therapy is experiential, just like the process and like training to be a better swimmer. Keep your heart in the lived-in experiences while keeping your eye on the prize.

Self-Reflection

1. Do you have any patterns in life where you experience less but think more? When and doing what?
2. Do you feel you get to experience the things in life that you wish, for example, traveling, hobbies and relationships?
3. How do you balance planning, thinking and analysing with experiencing? What do you find useful and when?

4. How much time do you find in therapy where you are thinking about doing or experiencing therapy vs analysing or focusing on the end goal rather than the process?
5. Do you experience the presence of the therapist or yourself in therapy?

What's the point now?

The statement, "What's the point of talking about it now? It's done; it's in the past," is a truism that often appears in therapy and in life. Something in the past has happened, maybe a trauma, abuse, familial issue, or divorce. The truth is that it has happened in the past and nothing can be done. A natural survival response may soon appear after a stressful situation because you need to function; you can't do anything about it and you just need to move on. It is such a common pattern in life that I suspect if someone said it, it would hardly ever go unchallenged.

However, from a psychological perspective, the mind and body can, in its survival mode, betray your wellbeing by leaving feelings undealt with "after the fact." Your feelings of hurt, confusion, sadness, anger and pain can be put in the back of your mind, pushed down, suppressed or even lost. Even if you were consciously aware, you may keep yourself occupied so not to face your feelings without even realising it. However, by forging on, you are taking money out of the bank of personal wellbeing, and eventually, you could be in debt without receiving any prior notification! The impact of "what's the point now?" could mean stress, anxiety, anger, feeling burnt-out or even panic and flashbacks, which are psychological meters of "something is not right." Psychological wounds, particularly deep ones, don't just disappear. In fact, they can become a dormant volcano. That does not mean every stressful or difficult event or your "norm" needs further work; it's just important too be open minded to the idea that there could be difficult psychological wounds unaddressed or dormant inside you.

Here is a narrative of a client who inadvertently hits a wound having "just moved on":

Sajidda came to therapy talking about her children's issues. They had been getting into trouble with the law, and she was feeling really guilty about not being a good mum. As she spoke, she brought her mum and dad to mind. Her mum was someone she had to protect rather than get support from, but her dad was a rock. As she said those words, her body shook and blood rushed to her head. A feeling for a grief not "grieved" pervaded the rest of her therapy.

In some cases, the scars may be obvious and you may not feel there is anything to do in therapy but to get on with it. However, exploring and processing it may lead you to feeling better, regardless of fixing the past, which you have no control of.

Therapy is a healing process and includes "processing" (See "But it's just talking"), so there is always a possibility, if that is something you want, to change how you feel in relation to the past, even though the past cannot be changed. It's a core part of healing in therapy, because nothing in the past can change, but you and your relationship with it can, if you're ready.

Self-Reflection

1. What are the most difficult events you have experienced?
2. How did you deal with them? Process them? Grieve your losses?
3. Do they impact your day-to-day life or inner world? How?
4. Are they something that relate to your problems in therapy?

Hitting a wall

Maybe at some point, whether it's after a session or two or even after months of smooth sailing, frustration or anger can build up towards therapy, the process and even the therapist. This may happen for many reasons, but one reason has to do with expectorations of therapy and the therapist.

Here are a few examples of how this "wall" can appear in therapy:

Sid spent the last few months really getting something from therapy. He always felt relieved after sessions, and even said, "I wish I had done this years ago." He had been talking about external matters that affected him in life. He had a general feeling about being "okay" with his situation, even to the point of acceptance, even though it was a difficult time for his family. His therapist was fairly directive at the beginning, even asking him some questions to help him understand for himself different perspectives. He would often turn to the therapist after speaking, coming away from his own thoughts as if looking outside for guidance and what to do or say in therapy.

However, after around 12 sessions, things started to change as the therapist gently stated "he had obviously been through a lot but also noticed that feelings were rarely talked about and he talked about serious issues without any emotion, like it did not happen to him." He had thought about it more and he tried to be more introspective and reflective about it, and silences were more frequent to allow for his own reflection. He continued as he had often done before turning to the therapist, for the therapist to speak or at the end of saying something.

It was then when given more space that words would not come out; for a few weeks, he felt gradually more and more frustrated until he finally stated his feelings. "I don't see the point of this therapy; I could do this at home, so why would I pay for it!" The therapist accepted this and was glad that his client was sharing his feelings. The therapist wanted to explain things but first wanted to create space to allow the situation's natural healing potential to be given time to be processed. The therapist simply said, "I am allowing you space to understand yourself. Is it okay if we hold on to this space and work with it?" That space generated new and important material into the process: why it's difficult to ask for help, how he did not feel the therapist was helping him and how he always felt on the "outside" of things. Although the process was challenging, and there was a risk that he would walk away from the process, the process was reinvigorated and the relationship strengthened. A barrier had been overcome and eventually, he felt better because of it, even though he did not know exactly why.

Another way frustration can come up also is when you feel you have talked about everything you can possibly talk about, and you feel you have purged everything but then nothing changes (See "But it's just talking?"). Maybe a moment comes and you turn to the therapist in the hope they will be able to move you forward; after all, you've said everything already. Maybe you wanted more from the therapist, an expectation that the therapist could guide you. The frustration builds but there is a chance for new doors to be unlocked, especially if the therapist and client can explore the frustration or loss of hope when this happens.

If you hit a wall, ask the therapist for help, and use the ideas in this book to help you.

Self-Reflection

1. What sort of things in life make you feel frustrated?
2. What is your usual way of dealing with frustration? For example, do you vent it to a friend or keep it in?
3. Do you feel safe so you can talk and vent your feelings if you feel frustrated in therapy?

Am I Stuck?

What do you do when you feel the therapeutic process is stuck or stagnating? You may experience stagnation after some time with the therapist or at various stages, even right from the beginning. You may even be aware of the reason why you're stuck, but feel powerless to take action because you don't know what to do. In most cases the therapist may already be aware of the stagnation and will be helping you in their own way, but as with all these ways you can take action too.

A sign that things are stagnating is when you feel that nothing is progressing, even after months of therapy, and you appear to be looping around similar content without insight or without experiencing a change. You have stopped learning and therapy feels flat, without energy or vitality; therapy could even be boring for you. On the other hand, you may still like going to therapy, and get a temporary release, but it's not producing the change you long for. It can feel easy, but you're stuck, nonetheless. You may even be using new techniques and tools, but nothing whirs inside you and you don't appear to be getting anywhere with it. It can feel like you're in a forest where no matter what direction you travel, it leads to the same point. When this happens it can be tempting to end therapy.

It is very difficult to give absolute guidance on how long it's okay to feel stuck in the hope that something may change. After all, even if you have felt stuck for many months or more, you could be just one session away from feeling less stuck and even getting a small or substantial breakthrough. Clients can feel stuck for a long time and eventually movement can happen, so there is no way for the amount of time to stay with the feeling of stagnation or when to leave. It is very difficult to give definitive advice on, other than if you are feeling that way, take some time to reflect upon it and take action.

Stagnation need not be seen as the end, especially because it can bring in new material and insight through exploring the nature of the stagnation itself. If you can pinpoint the source(s) of "stuckness", the underlying feelings and what has happened—or is happening—to bring it about, it could be a turning point in your journey. Understanding "stuckness" can open new doors.

Ultimately, on a path towards growth and healing, stagnation may be one of the many themes that underlie your difficulties. Therefore the feeling of being stuck should be embraced just as you can embrace other feelings, such as anger or guilt, to explore them rather than ignore them, as something that is wrong. However, left out of the room and out of your awareness, it can become the elephant in the room, unspoken but doing a lot to block your progress.

Therefore your stagnation becomes an important part of the therapeutic process, not a separate process. Telling the therapist you feel stuck may well be all you need to do to gain momentum in your process.

Strategies for working on stagnation

The reasons for feeling stuck are unique to you. Much of the work on exploring being stuck will require you to reflect inside yourself, your life and the relationship you have with the therapist. Although much of this book is geared around keeping your process going, and by implication not stagnating, here are some additional strategies for working with the feeling of stagnation.

Use the therapist
Talk to the therapist about your stuck feelings if you feel safe and are ready.

You can ask for a review of the progress against your aims and difficulties. You can use the review as a way of giving feedback to what you feel is missing and what you feel you need from the therapist. For example, you may feel you want more direction or even less direction, help with focusing the session or perhaps there are obstacles to you feeling safe and free in the relationship.

You can also ask the therapist what they feel about the process. Many therapists use their feelings about the process and the relationship to help you. For example, a therapist may feel they would like to know more of you, rather than just day-to-day activities, to get a sense of what is going on inside you. Others may reflect the question back to help you to consider the process more.

If you feel you would find it too difficult to talk about your feelings face to face, consider writing down your thoughts. You can send this to your therapist prior via secure email/message or take it with you to a session.

Explore the theme of "stuckness"
Relate stagnation to life in general and see if there are any similarities. For example, do you feel other parts of your life, such as work or relationships are stagnating? You can explore the nature of the stagnation, how and when it occurred, what is missing and why you feel it is occurring. If you find your life is stagnating or you have been through periods of historical stagnation then it may be well worth reflecting on, and drawing comparisons in the room. You can also relate feeling stuck to any similarities that come up from childhood, for example, lack of freedom, boredom, or lack of direction.

You can also use metaphors and imagery to express in as much detail as possible how "stuckness" feels. You can use pictures, drawings, and even stories to describe how you see stagnation. For example, you may relate stagnation to a plant that is not growing. By doing this type of expressive work you may be able to get closer to your underlying feelings and what's missing.

Another way of exploring stagnation is by reflecting on how you relate to it in therapy. For example, do you flow with it, get frustrated or even angry? Do you see it as part of the process or separate from it? Or did you expect it to happen as it's the norm in life and therapy?

Evaluate sources of "stuckness"
When evaluating the sources of "stuckness" you should not only look at yourself, but also consider whether it could be to do with the therapist too.

In evaluating the therapist, I would recommend going back to reflecting on their relational fit and whether or not you feel safe, and at ease within the relationship.

In evaluating yourself, you can look at how you apply yourself in therapy, and whether there is something you could change in your approach to it. For example, become more vulnerable, feelings-focused, or show more parts of your personality. I also recommend that you reflect on whether you have parts that are not ready to change and whether that contributes to or is causing the stagnation (See "You don't want change").

Alternatively, you may already be consciously aware of the possible reasons for why therapy is stuck. For example:

- Attraction or emotional dependency on the therapist (See "Love in the room").
- Difficulty sharing important information related to your problem.
- You want to be a good client and not disagree with the therapist
- There is an issue within the relationship. For example, a silent relational rupture based on a disagreement, hurt feelings, anger, or based on feeling criticised

Whatever you find or already know, if you feel safe and are ready, then you can explore what you know in therapy.

I hope the ways in this book will help you become unstuck, so do your fair share in therapy to keep your journey moving, however, that does not mean doing your "unfair share". If you have tried everything suggested, but something is still missing, you can think about leaving therapy. You have the right to end therapy and find someone else. If you do decide to end, you can explore your reasons for leaving your previous therapist with your current one and/or when beginning with the next therapist. Therapy is a journey, so you may encounter a number of therapists along the way. Moving on should be seen as a stepping stone rather than a failure.

Self-reflection

1. How long have you felt stuck in the process? Can you talk to the therapist? Is it a relational issue?
2. Does the feeling of being stuck seem familiar to past experiences, for example, those from childhood or in your current life?
3. What are the source(s) of "stuckness"? You may want to write in a journal, use art or have an internal dialogue to understand it better. For example, does it relate to:
   a. Lack of hope or meaning?
   b. Difficulty being vulnerable or showing all sides of yourself?
   c. Feeling safe and trusting the therapist?
   d. Feeling that the therapist judges you?
   e. Feeling the need to perform and be the "good client"?
   f. Are you worried about being vulnerable or getting into trouble?
4. What can the therapist do to help you? For example, be more directive or use several interventions.

But I lied!

In my experience of therapy coaching, clients can often be worried about changing their story, or revealing something important later on during the course of therapy. You may feel that doing so would be like being caught telling a lie, or you may have concerns about being criticised or blamed for doing so.

You may have worries that the therapist will think badly of you (say, because of having an affair). Or you may hide things because you fear you will not be believed, and sometimes you may hide things to avoid confronting your feelings and the truth.

Another reason for being selective is that you may hope that you can get what you need from therapy without going into the underlying issue. For example, anger management may be more about changing thoughts and behaviours around the anger rather than looking inside the anger, although a content-free therapy approach may be a way around this reluctance.

Of course, with a good therapist this is not the case at all, as it just represents who you are at a point in time. They are not lies or secrets. Your therapist knows that therapy is a process and your story can unfold in various directions, they are there to accept you as you are, not how you should be.

To help you understand how valid and normal it is to withhold or distort your truth here is a list of the most common distortions or concealments in therapy (Farber, A., 2019):

- Minimisation of impact including severity of symptoms
- Exaggeration of progress
- Suicidal thoughts, self-harm, and emotional distress
- All things sexual including history, fantasies and sex life
- Substance use and abuse
- Trauma
- Clinical progress and feelings about the therapist
- Insecurity about yourself
- Pretending to like therapists comments or suggestions
- Reasons for missed appointments or lateness
- Pretending therapy is more effective than it is
- Life regrets
- Pretending to do the homework
- Not saying you want to end therapy
- Something illegal
- Opinion of the therapist
- Feelings about your body

- Family secrets
- Things parents did that affected you

If any of these are relevant to your therapy and you are ready feel free to change the narrative.

Self-reflection

1. What are you beliefs about lying? Where did you get those beliefs from?
2. Is it okay to keep things back from relationships? What are the limits of sharing?
3. What would happen if you were found to lie? Both in past, present and therapy room?

So, you've come to therapy put in the work, done the "talking and feeling," but you wonder how all this "talking and feeling" could really be helpful, particularly as the past can't be changed and you still feel symptoms of panic. Surely, there is something more that you have to be doing to feel better? Well, not necessarily, unless of course things are stagnating or blocked (See "Am I stuck?") or the therapist is not right for you.

Here is a narrative from a client who cannot really understand how therapy could help:

"It's the past; I can't change nothing. It happened, you know. No matter how much talking I do, I can't change the fact that my mother did not want me. So, other than making me feel worse what is the point of being here?"

Therapists often talk about the client's "mind shift" or "shift" that brings about some change in relation to events, yourself, relationships and life, which in turn provides a way of feelings settled in your mind and body. Shifts come in many varieties – small, subtle, unnoticeable or large. Usually, shifts are small and subtle, hardly even noticeable, but these add up over time, and in many cases, you can feel better and may not know exactly why or what has happened. Therefore, the shift in the process can feel subtle or even mysterious.

Here are some excerpts of how clients felt and described their shift, which seemed in some ways not to make any sense:

John had found daily life hard to manage after the death of his brother. He spent four sessions in the darkness of pain, guilt and not wanting to accept his brother's death. On the fifth session, he came in, sat down, and said, "You know what? I feel a bit better but I don't really know why. I don't know why. What's happened?" It wasn't that he felt he had accepted the loss, but given the darkness he was in, it was almost a shock to him that he could in fact feel better able to function in life without knowing what he actually did! What he did was to be himself, as he was, someone grieving for a loss.

In this case, a client had worked over a year on her deep problems of rejection and abandonment from caregivers:

I don't know what has happened really, but I feel like I'm in a better place. Before, I used to feel so angry and sad being rejected or not cared about when I was developing relationships in groups, but now, although nothing has really changed, I feel I am stronger inside, and my hurt feelings don't feel as strong anymore. I could not have imagined this on its own would be enough."

Other times, a sudden insight, a "light bulb or "A-ha" moments can be the catalyst for change:

Whenever I get into a conflict with someone, I stick up for myself, and then I feel sorry for them as if I've done something wrong. I just want things to be okay and then I say "sorry," even though I don't feel I've done anything wrong. I do this so much. I even remember with my dad, whenever I didn't go along with what he said, he would sulk for days not talking to me and always... it was my mum who said to me, you need to sort it out and say sorry to dad. I always ended up saying sorry..... [A-ha...]

Another reason why change may sneak up on you is that small perceptual changes occur without being acknowledged or noticed. Feeling empowered in therapy, taking more time for yourself, less guilt of being out of work, sharing feelings, and talking about your problems to a partner provide small but incremental relief. All these layers of pressure can in themselves provide a backdrop to a sense of mental change, a shift and feeling more relieved.

From an outside perspective, it is easy to be surprised how therapy can in itself work, but don't underestimate therapy as being an answer to the unanswerable. Give it time and a place inside you, and you'll in most cases experience the shift for yourself. If you are working with a "good enough" therapist, have faith in the process before assuming this won't work. Regardless of how the shift occurs, whether it happens in awareness or out of awareness, it is a good sign that you're on your way. This could be a time to celebrate your hard work!

Self-Reflection

1. Do you understand why therapy is more than just talking?
2. Do you have examples of when you felt changed inside but you didn't know why?
3. Do you have examples of when you had a sudden "insight" into life or therapy?
4. If you feel therapy won't work, do you know the reasons why? Can you talk to a therapist about it?

Talking vs. Processing

Therapists often talk about processing, whether it is feelings, thoughts, images, body responses, memories or emotions. But what does that mean? How do I do that? And how will I be able to recognise the difference between talking on its own vs talking and processing? What does good "processing" look like?

Keyword: Process. In therapeutic terms, "process" can refer to three separate things: the steps and activities that occur during therapy that lead to growth, the process that is going on within you that has not been revealed or known about. Thirdly, in this section, the "process" refers to the characteristics of working on whatever comes up so it is effective in a therapeutic sense.

If you are talking about something, whether it's a situation, event, memory or even something that you have taken the brave step to disclose, this can be a critical first step and may be the most important step in your recovery. However, saying something out loud is usually just the beginning. Talking about something is not necessarily the same as completely processing it. Processing is to squeeze out all the healing potential, to be wrung dry and digested in to the psyche. For example, revealing a past mistake you feel guilty about is a start, but it won't necessarily enable the strong feelings, thoughts and beliefs you have about the mistake to be understood, dissipated, accepted or made less painful. To do so will require processing work with a therapist over time. So, processing in this sense is a mental conversion process, analogous to converting wheat to flour and eventually bread. You will need to combine ingredients to be able to process them and eventually to achieve healing. Identification of ingredients is a start, but it does not make the final product. Make new by processing in therapy.

Here is a narrative of someone who is either not ready to process something or they may even be aware that they are not doing it:

Jane had found it really hard to be vulnerable; her feelings were trapped inside. She made the brave step to share feelings. When she did, she did her best by quickly stating that "she found it hard, and even though she wanted to share more, she could not." It was understandable that was all she felt she could do, but it may not be enough to lift the block of "don't feel or share," even though she wished deep down that it was all she needed to do to recover from anxiety.

Kevin came into therapy for an addiction problem. He would spend most of the session talking about day-to day-things, stress, work and his addiction. He would spend most of the time talking about his symptoms, triggers, and how "if only" he could not drink anymore. Whenever he did talk about matters that stressed him, he would speak in generalities without going into specific examples and his deeper feelings. When he did talk about things, it would be about a situation that made him angry, but he spoke about a lot of things very quickly, moving from one situation to the next. It was clear he had feelings of anger and guilt but because he was not, for reasons unknown, processing his own thoughts and feelings, the process was looping rather than moving. So much content was being said, nothing really had a chance to be explored deeply, so he remained distant, like being read a book about someone else, not him.

So, what does good processing look like? To process something is to examine it, analyse it, and walk around it from different angles, like you would examine a statue for the first time. By processing through the feelings, the content and your relationship towards whatever is under examination, you can come to new awareness. In short, you give yourself the time to increase your understanding, to have new insights or to allow the feelings to pour out to help you. By processing feelings, memories and thoughts, you have the opportunity to uncover and give them a fresh look, updating your memories, joining the dots between the past and now, your understanding and their context. These insights can help you complete the "puzzle" in your story, moving your narrative and how you feel about yourself forward. Another way to see processing is that it is like clearing out a messy cupboard that needs reorganisation, checking the folders and files, and filing the files correctly in a way that makes sense to you; this helps you feel that things are in psychological order.

Here is an example extract of beginning processing in the case of Jane:

Therapist: Can you tell me more about the anxiety you felt when forcing yourself to tell me how you felt?

Client: .. I felt my heart pounding. It felt my body was pushing me back, and I could not speak.

Therapist. So, with those feelings, do you remember a time before when you had those same feelings of a pounding heart and something pushing you?

Client: [pausing ... hearing her breath change] It felt like a memory I have of my dad hitting me and telling me I was stupid and wouldn't be anyone and no one would want me. He physically pushed me back. I felt scared...

Sometimes, your patterns will be deeply ingrained and there will be good reason for that, whether it's fear of abandonment in relationships or a trauma of the past. These unconscious patterns that impact your life and cause issues can also be processed and brought into consciousness and understood. Insight can be gained and reinterpreted, so although the memories remain, the intensity of the pain and hurt settles down to a point where you can function in life.

Self-Reflection

- Are you used to exploring your thoughts and feelings about situations, e.g., to a friend or a partner?
- How much vulnerability do you typically show? Do you share how events affected you? Or do you find it harder to share feelings when you may be perceived to be less in control, weak, vulnerable or fragile?
- How do you feel when you share feelings or have had to share them last? Do you feel you avoid or block feelings, find them difficult or even scary?

It doesn't make sense

At the beginning, unless it's a specific life event, confusion may reign over your problems—a mist over something, hiding it from view. Your problems may seem illogical, like being struck down with an illness without a reason or a "cure."

However, bring in enough insight and everything will begin to make sense; "you" will make sense, your truth will emerge, and you will be able to tell your story. What appears illogical will have logic. There is virtually always a reason for difficulties, and when there is not, you can work with what you do know.

Often clients seek answers to questions either explicitly or implicitly. Here are some examples of questions that may be asked during therapy:

- Why do I feel down?

- Why do I feel anxious when talking about myself?

- Why do I find it difficult to change?

- Why am I angry at the therapist?

- What purpose did my addiction serve?

- Why did my uncle abuse me?

- Why do I feel guilty saying "no?"

- Why am I scared that the therapist will think I am making things up?

- Why do I find it difficult to share what I feel about the therapist?

- Why do I have panic attacks in work meetings?

- … Add any number of "why" questions.

Here is an example where Joe feels stuck, because he doesn't understand his anger:

Joe had been in therapy for six months. He felt "rage" whenever he felt deceived by others. He would talk about what happened and about what he felt, but nothing that came out of therapy changed him. He was frustrated that although he had understood the dynamic of feeling that people were trying to dominate him, it only triggered more vengeful anger inside him. He would often exclaim, "This does not make sense!" He tried logically thinking about "everyone's entitled to an opinion," or "I can't control others, only influence them," but his pattern was ingrained and continued. It was as if something was missing from view, but he didn't know what.

As you take the therapist on a journey inside your experiences you can start to gain an understanding of what's wrong—the underlying patterns and beliefs that contribute to the problem you are working on. You'll understand the purpose they served and how they hinder your life goals now. In short you'll understand your truth. Depending on what you're trying to figure out you cannot usually just arrive at an answer or an insight without expanding your awareness through the therapeutic process.

For example, Joe spent six months understanding his feelings of anger and where they may have originated from, and then taking time to process his feelings, and understand the source(s) of his pain.

Although there a lot of nuances in Joe's story he came to an understanding of "how" and "why" from talking about his hostile parental environment. He realised that during his childhood he had had no personal power, and felt his father and mother preferring his siblings to him. He was able to bring out his truth, and realise that his true "source" of pain was in the theme of being "belittled" while growing up.

By understanding this story, and that the patterns of the past continued to apply now, he was able to get to a point where he could differentiate between "past" and "present" feelings. Joe continued to work on his feelings and over time he was able to reduce the frequency and intensity of anger whenever he felt deceived.

At other times what's wrong comes out from nowhere, you're in the midst of exploring events and you encounter a sudden flash of insight. Here Jenny describes her problem and stumbles upon an insight.

[Jenny] Whenever I get into a conflict with someone, I stick up for myself, and then I feel sorry for them as if I've done something wrong. I just want things to be okay and then I say "sorry," even though I don't feel I've done anything wrong. I do this so much. I even remember with my dad, whenever I didn't go along with what he said, he would sulk for days not talking to me ... it was my mum who said to me, you need to sort it out and say sorry to dad. I always ended up saying sorry..... [A-ha...]

Jenny has joined the dots and come to a realisation that because of her own past experiences of having to say sorry, she continued to do so in the present. The reoccurring pattern of "It must be my fault" came to the fore and she could relate that to a number of relational difficulties as an adult.

Building an understanding of patterns in life, and why these patterns began can be likened to trying to complete a complex and multidimensional jigsaw puzzle. It's a puzzle no one really gets to totally complete, just like learning any complex subject never finishes, but with enough of the pieces in place you can have a pretty good idea of what the picture represents. Obviously, with more pieces, you will gain a deeper understanding, but as long as you develop the appropriate areas of the jigsaw, you'll be moving your process along. With insight you come to understand why you are the way you are, sort out what's useful, and thus what change you want to work on.

So, next time you find something confusing or you don't understand, see if you can make the illogical logical. There is always a reason.

Self-Reflection

1. Do you often feel like you don't know why you feel a certain way?
2. What feelings exist in your life that feel like you don't understand why they are happening, for example, anxious, feeling low, emotional, angry, etc.?
3. How long has this been happening? If this has been happening for a long time since childhood, what factors would have contributed to your current unknown feelings? Consider writing your life story to see if it reveals any new ideas.
4. Do you have some examples? For each example, write about what was happening 5 days before the situation and whether there were any stresses or triggers. Remember, stresses may be a lack of a need, e.g., feeling lonely.

Therapists work with you as you are. Just bring you and they will accept whatever you bring in as the starting point to therapy. Being nervous arriving for therapy is a normal response; after all, it is something new, and it may be exciting heralding a new chapter in life.

However, attending therapy can be worrying and anxiety-provoking for many. Your feelings may relate to fear of the unknown, what you will learn, being emotionally triggered and being judged by the therapist. You may also have "performance anxiety" of therapy and feel that you need to do therapy right and are worried you'll not be able to express yourself and say what you need to say. Underlying that may be a feeling of "am I good enough for the therapist or to do what is needed to heal?"

Although you may feel that way, the safe environment of therapy with a "good enough" therapist isn't anything like your fears and anxieties you have about therapy. The therapist is there to accept you, not judge you, to empathise and understand your world. Therapists are not there to say that you are wrong or defective, to shame or criticise you. They are there to work with you. In fact, therapy is about enabling you to be "as you are" regardless. They will welcome you and invite you to be as you are, regardless of your nerves, anxieties and worries. The therapist accepts whatever it is you think, feel, say or don't say, your symptoms, even if those feelings are directed towards them.

They will work with whatever you present to them. So, being as you are is welcome. You can express whatever it is if you can. For example, if you express that you feel the therapist may judge you, they will work with that. If you feel anxious, they will work with that; if you don't want to talk, they will work with that; if you feel you don't want to share, that is okay too. Of course, you may wish to share all those anxieties, worries and feelings, and it can be beneficial, but you are autonomous and free to choose.

This does not mean that therapist won't gently challenge you or doesn't care, but they do so in a way that will help you with your problems and goals. Therapists don't have a preconception of how you should be and from that point, anything is possible. Just bring yourself, as you are and however you want to present yourself in therapy.

Here is a narrative of someone who was being himself, regardless of not being able to show all of himself to the therapist. It is not wrong; it is right.

For a number of sessions, Dave had taken charge in therapy and worked with efficiency through his issues, finding solutions and answers. However, it was only when he let go of the mask of "being in control and knowing the answer" that the therapist got to know and understand him more. Deep down, he felt a need to hide that part of him that felt "depressed" and "not understood." He was presenting part of himself, rather than the whole. He began showing who he was rather than what he ought or thought he should be in the room.

Of course in therapy, you may not know who you are. You are likely to discover that as a natural consequence of therapy, and so who you are in therapy is also likely to change as the process unfolds. However, being as you are means it doesn't matter how you are it will be accepted. Be real, unreal or wear a mask, or an ideal. Be compliant, defiant, or quiet. There is no mandatory version of yourself you must bring. It's all okay and acceptable (as long as it's not harmful of course!).

Self-Reflection

1. Do you feel you can be you? Reflect on differences between work, family, social, therapy or other activities.
    a. Carrying multiple personas (or masks) is a normal way for us to be. We may present ourselves very differently depending on the situation.
2. What are the different types of mask you wear in different settings?
3. Ideally what type of persona would you like to carry most of the time?
4. If you feel you can't be you a lot of the time, reflect on reasons why.
5. What persona(s) do you carry in therapy or in different settings? Here are a few ideas:
    a. The Good Client
    b. The Appeaser or Pleaser
    c. Joker
    d. Hero/Anti Hero
    e. Rational/Logical or Emotive
    f. Professional
    g. Controlled
    h. Romantic
    i. Independent/Self Sufficient

But my life's still the same

Where appropriate, putting things you've learnt into action alongside your development in therapy provides the reciprocal feedback loop to growth both in therapy and in your life.

It can be essential depending on what you're working on in targeting external tasks, activities and goals alongside the work you do in therapy. This can have the effect of catalysing your process because you can begin to build confidence in being able to overcome difficulties and achieve life goals.

Here is a possible consequence of not taking action from your learning in therapy:

Hussan had been coming to therapy for some time. He felt he had understood himself better and had come to peace in respect of his difficult feelings for his mother who had caused him to feel worthless through neglect.

Hussan had learnt that part of him was still feeling neglected, and what he really needed was more attention and care. But he had not put into practice any way in which he could have a chance of receiving care. He continued to devote time to work, but did little if anything to develop the relationships he craved for.

Hassan become aware of his inactivity outside of therapy and began taking steps:

In the next session, Hussan appeared to be taking a small but important steps towards what he really needed, he said, "After last week, I started putting myself out there more. I allowed myself to chat with people. I even messaged someone I see at the gym a lot and asked him how a meeting went with his manager. It felt good—baby steps, as they say."

In therapy, you're learning about yourself and what you need, and that may require taking action outside of the therapeutic process. If it's a relationship you need, you can start to focus on being relational; if you want to have more passion towards work, you can start devising a plan to get you there, and if you feel insecure about your relationship, it may be time to talk.

Taking action doesn't just mean visible action, it could mean consciously trying to have a different frame of mind. For example, being more aware of feelings or being kinder to yourself.

Here are some examples of putting what you learn or need into action:

- If you're anxious about doing things on your own, take a small step by sitting in a coffee shop with a coffee and a laptop.
- If you want friendships, join an events group where you share the same interests as the members.

- If you want to improve your relationship with your partner, talk more about your feelings with them
- If you want a hobby, pick one and try it.
- If you are overstretched, plan some self-care.
- If you tend not to hold boundaries, learn to be more assertive.
- If you want to be more vulnerable, start sharing deeper feelings (safely of course!)
- If you want to overcome a fear of birds then you'll need to set yourself some exposure tasks (with the therapist's help).

If you find there is something blocking you from putting something you have learned or something that you need into action then talk to your therapist to understand it more. For example, is it a fear of the consequences or do you just need help coming up with tasks to apply? Remember, you don't have to take big steps, just take the steps you can safely make.

Taking action is a way of taking responsibility for yourself, by being the good parent that teaches you to look after yourself. So focus on putting things you've learnt into action—when you're ready of course.

Self-Reflection

1. Is there anything you've learnt in therapy that you may need to put into action?
2. What are your needs in life? Do you need to work on them outside of therapy?
   o *Needs can be basic survival, food and water, socialising, belonging, friends, life partner, love and care, having a passion or a purpose.*
3. Now, write about your action-based goals. You can start from easiest and work towards the hardest if it helps.

Therapy is not always a straight line, nor is it without difficulty. You may feel worse before feeling better. A narrative of someone who feels worse:

"I wasn't expecting this. I feel worse than I did at the start. This can't be good! Every time I come here, I'm more and more in touch with the pain of my wife cheating on me! It just stirs things up more."

Well, it's an understandable sentiment that getting in touch with pain is difficult. It is a bit like exposing an open wound to the air or putting you hand near the fire you'll want to be cautious. However, it could be also be a significant sign that therapy is working and on your way to feeling better longer-term.

There are a number of reasons why you may feel worse, but essentially, you're getting in direct contact with your feelings and thoughts, which may be difficult to face and which may include bad memories, grief and other emotions that were previously hidden from your immediate attention (or suppressed, as therapists refer to it).

"My dad died 12 months ago and we didn't really have a relationship. He would never really make the effort. I always had to make the effort for him to come around. I'm okay because he wasn't there for me at the start and was never there so it's not like having a real dad. There is nothing I can do about it; I just have to accept it."

Here, a client is starting to touch upon something early on that could be, unbeknown to him, a set of complex painful feelings underneath that are causing his downward spiral into depression. Once revealed, the painful emotions can come to the surface, such as feeling rejection and guilt for losing the father he never really had.

In some cases, the pain could be totally hidden until associated memories come up that you did not even know existed. In the excerpt below, the client has realised a painful memory he had "forgotten," and getting in touch with the feelings of being abused made him feel worse and even more ashamed at first but he had made the first step.

"I had a good childhood. But I remember always being the one who listened; no one appeared to listen to me about my feelings. I just became a listening robot to get attention and fit in. One day, I was coming home from school, and a bunch of kids attacked me. I remember going home in shock and for some reason, I don't know why, I never told anyone. I was so ashamed. It's only after talking about it that this memory came to me."

Once the therapeutic process brings these hidden or untouched feelings out to the fore to be worked on, you can feel worse because you're now feeling parts of the original pain and the feelings surrounding them, which brings an opportunity for healing.

"Feeling worse" in therapy can appear to be self-defeating or hopeless, when in fact, it could be the opposite. The therapeutic journey should not be seen as a straight line but more as a road with many contours, turns, and twists. You could be well on your way to feeling better and you just don't know it yet. So, if you get into this situation, you should not just ask, am I feeling better, but also is it working? I also recommend not leaving the therapist without exploring the "worse feeling" first. Sticking with the process, working through the difficult feelings could be the path of recovery you just might need.

Warning. *We have to caveat this section a bit. If you're not ready to go deeper into your feeling, then you are not ready. It has to be what you want to do. Also, just because you're feeling worse or if more pain is being experienced, this does not imply that it's healthy either. Talk to your therapist and/or physician if you have concerns and you are feeling worse.*

Self-Reflection

1. What are you past experiences of feeling worse with regard to your physical or emotional wellbeing? What did you learn from it? Do you see a pattern of how you deal with difficulties in life and in your mental wellbeing?
2. If you have felt worse after a session or for a while during therapy, can you pinpoint possible explanations as to why that is?
    a. Tip: in general, therapy can be very exhausting and draining. Working on feelings you are facing anew or having to delve into them can be straining. On the other hand, it can be very lifting. What do you normally experience?

But I'm feeling better now!

Alison attended a couple of sessions. On the third, she sat down and said:

"I feel better now. I went through the reasons for my anxiety and don't think I will need more therapy after today. I need to focus on helping others who rely on me at work."

Sure, therapy can work wonders and one session can be enough. Of course, respecting your feelings is important too and that is a good sign; it may be a sign you're on the right path and it may be you don't need any more therapy.

On the other hand, be mindful of your better feelings being at the surface level only. You've probably experienced an illness that has kept you in bed and then we can feel that little spark where we seem to be on the mend, only to discover later we needed more time to recover before getting back to a normal routine. Similarly, for stressful, complex or long-lasting issues, be open to the idea that more work and time for healing may be needed. This is akin to feeling like symptoms are disappearing but it is masking a lot more issues under the surface.

Alison had a couple of weeks off therapy and then decided to return.

"You know, I'm really frustrated with myself. I was getting better but I had three or four times when I just broke down crying; it came out of nowhere. Maybe I'm not feeling as good as I thought yet. I don't know whether I should continue. What do you think?"

Here, in between sessions, Alison had come to realise that she did benefit from a few sessions and certainly her symptoms appeared manageable and she felt lighter in herself, but it was temporary relief, akin to taking a painkiller when you need surgery. Take heart, this is a good step. It is not uncommon in therapy to feel worse before feeling better or even to feel better and then feel worse. Give yourself time, even if it means more recovery time. This is an investment in you.

Self-Reflection

1. What are you past experiences of feeling better, whether in life, physical or emotional wellbeing? What process do you normally follow? What did you learn from it? Do you see a pattern of how you deal with difficulties in life and your mental wellbeing? For example, do you tend to want to push through or do you get anxious when you are taking time to recover?
2. If you have felt better to only feel worse later after a session or after being in therapy for a while, can you pinpoint possible explanations as to why that is?
3. Are there areas in your life you feel you're not ready to address in therapy?

I think im dependent

There are all sorts of dependencies such as chemical substance, an addictive or toxic relationship, a hobby or work. Clearly, dependency can get out of hand when you are controlled by the dependence. But what about dependency on therapy and even the therapist? Contrary to popular belief, it is perfectly acceptable for you to feel transitory dependence on therapy and the therapist. You may feel that therapy is where you feel most cared for and understood, and you may feel the relief and reward of coming to therapy.

Consider the following statements from clients:

"Therapy is all I have right now. I don't have any support, friends, or family; I'm alone. I really need this... I'm so glad I have got you..."

"I am using the therapist in my mind outside of therapy for support and inner dialogue...I am glad to have them as an inner resource for support"

"[Inner voice] ... I feel so cared for by you... I wish I could be with you more. I love being near you... I can't think of anywhere else I'd rather be."

All these feelings are valid, after all, therapy is a place for you to draw out your feelings, needs, and desires in whatever shape or form you choose. So although dependence may be there for you, unlike an addictive substance, it does not have to be one that controls you. Therapy will come to an end, and you'll want to be able to safely withdraw from it when the time is right.

If your dependence feels very strong, perhaps based on emotions and/or an attraction; you feel you need them more and more, and are worried about the effects of ending, I recommend speaking to the therapist. If you cannot speak to the therapist you can seek further support.

Self-Reflection

If you feel dependent or are struggling to end even though you have met your goals, what are the reasons? Possible reasons include:

1. You really like having a safe place to talk.
2. You feel like you would be alone or more alone without the relationship with the therapist.
3. You feel anxious that problems have not been resolved yet and wonder what you will do if they come back.
4. The relationship with the therapist is strong and you would miss it.
5. You find it hard to tell the therapist for fear of upsetting them or being criticised for leaving.
6. Dependence or love attraction to the therapist.

Slip away

You can end silently if you wish, without talking about endings. It is not that uncommon for people to stay silent about their plan to end, even if it feels like they have achieved their aims.

Here is a way of understanding silent endings from a therapist's perspective:

A client had been seeing me for a number of months. I felt the relationship to be good and he said that he was starting to feel better; it felt like an ending could be on the horizon.

For a number of weeks he sent me a text messages asking to rearrange planned sessions to which I replied with possible options. However, I noticed after a few weeks, there were longer time spaces between messages and eventually, after a few times trying to arrange a session, messages stopped coming in altogether. He ended silently; the messages just stopped coming.

From my perspective, he has autonomy and freedom to choose the ending. It is what he needed at the time—he got what he needed and ended silently, I wished him the best in my heart. I also wondered why he felt the need to silently end. I reflected on the multiple losses he had suffered in his family recently and whether they linked to not wanting another ending, however positive. I would never know for sure. I also wondered whether he had ever felt a need to end, or even whether he had good role models that showed him a good "goodbye".

The other part of me wondered whether it would have been something to explore, as part of his process. His need was to end in the way he did; as a therapist, this wasn't about my needs.

This example demonstrates two differing perspectives: a reason for ending silently and a reason for working actively towards an ending. Maybe the client felt he did not want to go through another ending given the losses he had suffered, and the therapist wondering whether a process of ending could have been another way of mourning the losses, or experiencing a better ending in order to celebrate and say goodbye.

Ultimately, unless the therapist initiates the end, you're free to choose to end—for the reasons you believe are right and in a manner which you feel is suitable. You should not feel you must have a formal ending—one in which you say goodbye. It's not uncommon for clients to decide to leave without really saying why or to feel they need a formal ending.

There is no right or wrong answer, it's about what you need. You decide.

Therapist initiated ending

If a therapist ends with you they should be able to justify it and give enough time for a graceful end. Endings can surface feelings, such as frustration, rejection and sadness, and the therapist should be able to work with your feelings in relation to the prospect of ending.

In this example, a client has expressed anger towards the therapist for the ending:

Client: I'm angry with you for ending therapy. It feels like you've given up on me.

Therapist: I'm glad you feel safe enough to share your feelings and for letting me know you're not happy with me. What I am hearing is you are feeling rejected by me. But I promise you, that's not the case. If I were to keep you here in therapy, and I can't help you, I would not be doing the right thing. I care because I want you to get the right support. With your PTSD, I believe someone who specialises in this would be able to help you more at this stage. Does that make sense?

Naturally there could be plenty more to explore about the ending, such as the feeling of being "given up on". Good therapists, time willing, would help you work through those feelings when they end therapy.

Of course, if a therapist has ended abruptly, say through an email, that is not acceptable professional practice unless there has been a force majeure incident. Sudden endings by the therapist are usually rare but I do hear of them; I recommend you talk to your therapist if you are worried that they will abruptly end with you.

If you are in distress due an abrupt ending, seek further support.

Endings are Therapy

So what's all this about endings anyway?

What if you had to stop a really good film before the ending?
What if you listened to your favourite piece of music and stopped it in the middle?
What if you watched an exciting sporting competition but never knew the result?
How would you feel?

Now. How would you feel..
If you never got to say what you wanted to say to someone you cared about?
If you never got to say how someone hurt you?
If you never got to say goodbye to a friend?
If you never got to say goodbye to someone who supported you?
If someone you loved said they wanted to say something important, but never got a chance?

Would it bother you? For many people the answer is yes because these situations are all to do with having feelings, and facing issues or concerns. But for others the thought of endings can be painful, scary and an anxiety-inducing experience. Ending may be embraced, or avoided, feelings expressed or left unsaid; either way endings will happen whether or not we choose to experience them directly.

The prospect of ending, whether imagined or initiated by you or your therapist can bring to the surface a variety of feelings. Here are some possible feelings as you contemplate endings:

- I will know when to end.
- I'll feel indifferent to ending.
- I'm anxious the therapist is going to dump me.
- I didn't like what the therapist said so I'm going to end it (whether imagined or followed through).
- I want to leave but I don't know how.
- I don't know what I'll do without therapy. I'll really miss it.
- I don't want this relationship to end. I'll really miss my therapist.
- I don't know if I'll get more from staying or from leaving.
- Should I leave this therapist and try another?
- I would feel guilty for leaving, especially after all the work we've done.
- I don't want to leave my therapist because they'll be losing an income stream.
- I am scared of losing my therapist. Last time they were late, I nearly had a panic attack.

Therapists are typically taught to keep endings in mind during the process so that they can be aware of your needs, and so that you are ready for it when it arrives. However, you can also help yourself by airing your feelings about endings during the process, or when you're thinking about initiating the ending. Feelings about endings can interfere with your process and / or they can be used as an opportunity to catalyse it. For example, if you imagine the therapist is going to "dump" you, it could be a hindrance in therapy because you aren't able to be yourself, or it could be an opportunity for exploration if you're struggling to find your authentic voice.

Endings are not separate to therapy: they are therapy. Your feelings, or even lack of feelings, and how they relate to your past can all be used therapeutically. Thinking about endings is also a way of determining whether you are really ready to end.

Exploring experiences of endings

Your life experiences of endings can also be another therapeutic source to explore. You can reflect upon your experiences of endings and how you have dealt with them. Here are some examples of life experiences related to endings:

- My husband left me and my children for my friend.
- I had a miscarriage. This is my fifth.
- We lost our family home.
- I usually slip away quietly at the end of a training course and don't like to say goodbye.
- I have lost all my family and friends now. I am the only one left.
- My father abandoned me when I needed him.
- I always say goodbye after meeting people at the end of a training course and make sure I take some contact details.
- I can end easily, sometimes I think too easily, without much reflection, even after years of knowing someone.
- My two brothers died in the space of six months.
- I am used to people leaving me.
- My friend passed away and I wasn't allowed to attend their funeral. I vowed never to have a best friend again.
- I've left the life of a bachelor behind.
- I saw my dog get run over and he died in my hands.
- I loved to dance but after my injury I couldn't dance again.

By reflecting upon your experiences of endings, you can understand what they mean to you: your underlying beliefs, and how you would have liked endings to happen, including therapy. It is not necessary to have a particular concern about endings, but it may increase your self-understanding about how you work and why.

A common theme linked with endings is not knowing if it is the right time to end. Sometimes you end for rational, well thought-out reasons, such as you don't feel the therapist is right for you, you feel worse or you're just not ready for therapy. Whenever you decide to end therapy, regardless of the reasons, you can reflect on your reasons or talk with the therapist.

But when is it time to end in the recovery phase of therapy? You know you have improved, even beyond what you thought achievable, but you can still be left feeling confused, guilty, or even anxious about whether to continue or to end.

Sometimes it can be about the transition out of a good relationship, or you feel you may still need the therapist; after all, what if your problem or symptoms return? Other times, it could be that you'll miss having a space in which to be heard.

I would suggest giving yourself time and space to work through these feelings, ideally with the therapist, and then eventually you will be able to answer the question of whether you are ready to end or not.

A common strategy used to test out whether you are ready to end, is to allow more time between sessions, reducing session frequency and taking a break for a few weeks. If you're worried about needing the therapist you can ask about their policy if you need to return. You're likely to find that therapists, particularly in private practice, will welcome you back as long as they have availability.

Ultimately, if you're not sure, or you have strong feelings about the ending, then that can be a sign you're not ready and need to do more work before making the decision to end.

The good goodbye

If you're ready and feel safe I recommend a defined ending stage with the therapist, regardless of whether you or the therapist initiates it. The ending stage could be for five minutes, a single session or many sessions over months. If you're not used to experiencing endings, or are used to bad endings, this is a chance to change that history. An ending can be therapeutic, because it's an opportunity to say what you feel, what the ending meant and to gain closure.

Here is an example of feelings experienced towards the end:

I feel excited, nervous, happy, and a little sad, but because of therapy I can cope with them. I'm a little sad because it feels like I'm losing a friend. I'm nervous because I don't know what the future holds. I'm also happy that my leaps and gains are far more than I could have ever hoped for. It's time to trust myself and try on my own. It's the beginning of a new chapter for me.

Here are some ideas for reflection during the ending stage of therapy:

- Your readiness to allay any concerns you may have about ending.
- Your journey, such as highlights, lowlights and turning points.
- What you found useful or not during the process.
- Your previous experiences of endings in contrast to therapy ending.
- What if feels like to end the relationship with the therapist.
- What your plans are after therapy.
- What your learnings were during the process.
- What else you would like to work on.
- How you like to end things.
- What this way of ending feels like.

Endings, especially if you have a strong relationship with your therapist can be emotion filled. However, by the end you should be ready to move to your next stage, either in life or even to another therapist. If you feel like it's a milestone then celebrating the ending together can be a gift.

Self-Reflection

1. Are endings important to you at all? Do endings worry you?
2. How have endings been for you in the past, for example, work, school, university, relationships, partners, friends, bereavement, and loss of any sort?
3. Have you had bad endings?
4. If you meet a new group of people in a workshop, event or in training for a few days or weeks, how do you generally say goodbye?
5. What would a good ending look like for you?
6. What are your thoughts and feelings about your relationship with the therapist? Would it be difficult to end?
7. Would you like to end silently or experience the ending?
8. What would you like to talk about or do during your ending with the therapist?

In this chapter, I explore themes that could surface as a result of your relationship with the therapist.

Maybe you feel the therapist is "paid to care", that they keep interrupting you, or perhaps you feel they are critical of you. As with all the themes in this book, not all will be applicable to you, but if any resonate, then that is a good opportunity for further self-reflection and potential work with the therapist (including repairing the relationship or aborting therapy).

Why your feelings about the therapist could be important?

Are you coming into therapy where relationships are in the foreground of the work? Then it can be useful for you to reflect upon and talk to your therapist about what you feel about your relationship with them, and compare and contrast that with any other relational difficulties you experience.

How you feel about the therapist can be really useful "live" information into the therapy room, particularly if you feel your problems are relational in nature. For example, want to improve your relationships, work on connecting more with friends or to find a partner? I really recommend writing down how you feel about the therapist and the relationship. If it makes sense, link your feelings towards your therapist and to that of other relationships, including caregivers, to see if it can open new doors for exploration in or out of the therapy room.

Here are some ways people may experience their therapeutic relationship:

- You idealise the therapist. There are two particular patterns that frequently occur when clients think about the therapist being ideal. The first is that the therapist needs to *be* the ideal meeting a near perfect expectation; the second is the therapist *is* the ideal! In the former clients are dissatisfied because the therapist doesn't meet ideal expectation and the later they are idolised as being near perfect.
- You keep the therapist away. You inadvertently keep the therapist away from helping you fully usually out of your own awareness. For example, by not acknowledging their care or contribution.
- You want to be "the good client." You not only want to perform or do well in therapy but a lot of that is related to pleasing the therapist.
- You feel a deep feeling of dependence on the therapist, which may include emotional, romantic or erotic dependence. They occupy a large part of your mental space, thus interfering with your therapeutic goals.
- Your feel indifferent or nothing about the therapeutic relationship. They occupy none or little of your mental space.

- You don't particularly like the therapist and have negative feelings towards them.
- You see them as better than you in some way e.g. more attractive, competent, academic which interferes with your process.
- You feel the therapist is judging you even though rationally there is no reason to feel that way.
- You feel you really miss the therapist and therapy between sessions, but you feel its healthy and balanced. You feel the therapist cares about me and I care about them too.
- You think your therapist is okay but not sure if they really care or whether they are faking it to be paid.
- You are not sure if the therapist cares really; they have so many clients, so why should I matter?

Here are some ways you can open up exploring this topic with the therapist:

- "I heard there are patterns in how we relate to people based on past experiences"
- "I wonder whether there are similarities I can explore here with you?"
- "I wish to compare relationships in general to our relationships. Is that okay?"

How you feel about the therapist, whether positive, neutral or negative could be influenced by your learnt experiences. For example, if you have had bad experiences with men all your life, it may interfere with you feeling safe. There is nothing wrong with feeling that way, but it's better to be aware of it and explore it with them. You can also use this knowledge when finding a therapist.

Self-Reflection

- Have you historically or are currently experiencing relational issues?
- Are relationships important to you in life? What type?
- What is your ideal type of friend? Or partner?
- Do you make connections with people easily?
- Does money get in the way of trusting the relationship?
- Do you feel you struggle to make connections with people?
- Do you often feel disappointed with relationships? If so, why?
- Do you generally find after meeting a number of therapists, you cannot feel a connection with the therapist even after several attempts? Why do you believe that is? Are there any parallels between how you feel with therapists and other relationships?
- Do the answers to these questions change what qualities you look for in a therapist?
- Do you want to talk about your feelings with the therapist?

There are two particular patterns that frequently occur when clients think about the therapist. The first is the therapist needs to *be* the ideal; the second is the therapist *is* the ideal!

In the first sense of needing the therapist to live up to an ideal, remember the therapist does not have to be perfect or indeed tick all your boxes; they just need to be "good enough." I use the term "good enough" throughout this book but what does "good enough" really mean? The phrase "good enough mother" was termed by a British psychoanalyst, D.W. Winnicott. He coined the term to express the idea that while a mother starts by sacrificing her needs to fulfill her child's, such as sleep, later in development, the mother allows for small frustrations, for example, a delay in responding as the child starts to cry. She is not "perfect" but she is "good enough" in that the child only feels a slight amount of frustration, which gives the child space to learn about her place in the world and to develop. I refer to the term "good enough therapist" throughout this book to allow for that development. The therapist may not always be attuned to your needs in the room. A good therapist is never able to be "perfect" at all times or know what is going on or what you need, but they can be "good enough," which is not only realistic but it may even be an important part of your healing.

In the second sense, the therapist *is* the ideal. You may hang on everything the therapists says; they represent the perfect therapist or the perfect imagined caregiver, partner or friend. Whatever they do and say is golden; they are golden. While that can be a great sign that you have a good relationship with the therapist and they are competent, it is also an opportunity to understand what is going on as these feelings may mean more than what appears to be apparent. However, what does it mean in reality? Does it in reality mean you see others as more important, more competent and better that you? Does it mean you want to please or be a good client? Or is it that they fill a need, such as a good role model or someone who cares and provides love?

If you have become aware of this pattern in other relationships, write it down and identify if anything comes up you can explore with the therapist. It may be useful to relate these feelings to your self-worth, which is how you judge yourself. While there are external things, like work satisfaction, that can build your self-worth, the type of self-worth people often have difficulty with is self-judgement, which is not tied entirely with external achievements, such as personal success, wealth or being appreciation. Self-worth is a deeper sense of judgement and feelings about yourself, such as feeling damaged, unworthy of love, abandoned, or self-loathing. These themes can remain static, having been "created" in our history of childhood, culture, family relationships, school and society. For example, feeling secure with your parents and being able to explore and make mistakes is going to be positive for your self-worth, but being persistently scolded, abused, and bullied and having a lack of feelings of belonging in the world is not a recipe for good self-worth.

Here is an example of a client idealising the therapist:

Karim came to therapy and had a good relationship with the therapist. He would often compliment the therapist, "You must be so good with being assertive with people," "You have so many qualifications,", "You always seem to calm me down." However, he was putting the therapist on a podium, and wanted to follow the therapist's lead, looking for the therapist's judgements, even by trying to read his body language. When the therapist shared his feelings about it, the client said "Well, I want to know what you think and what you need me to say." The therapist replied, "I appreciate that you have faith in me and in the process, but I'm sitting here thinking, it would be nice to hear about you, what you feel and what you want to talk about." In this case, Karim was so focused on the therapist, he had not yet developed the trust in himself to know the answers from inside himself.

Whether you see the therapist as an ideal, less than ideal, or want them to be the ideal and these feelings interfere with therapy, you will likely want to explore it further.

Self-Reflection

1. Were your caregiver's ideal? Why?
2. Do you tend to attach or value others' opinions and knowledge more than your own? Under what circumstances?
3. When you idealise, have you ever been disappointed, feeling they did not meet the ideal standard?
4. If applicable, what is the impact of you not feeling self-worth? Do you feel the therapist has good self-worth? Is this something to explore in therapy?

Gareth had met the woman of his dreams, she was smart, successful and so caring. Gareth held her tightly in his mind, first thing in the morning, at work and at night. People noticed how distracted he was, but he didn't care because he was in love. As long as she was with him, he would never need again. He lived to see her and counted the days and hours till their next meet. The only problem, it was his therapist and he knew he needed to leave her but could not. He was dreading her next two week break.

The foundation of therapy is built upon the relationship you have with your therapist, which on the whole is empathic, accepting and caring. The building of this foundation takes place over time as you start to feel, to varying degrees, safer, stronger, deeper, and more connected. This is really healthy and shows the work you're both putting in. It is also quiet natural that feelings arise within you, where you do feel a sense of care or even love towards the therapist. If you chose them proactively, it's likely there must have been something that "attracted you" to them. These feelings can be mutual and respectful with boundaries, and they have the power to fuel your healing process.

You may also encounter stronger emotional, romantic and sexual feelings towards your therapist. These feelings may also be familiar to you, resembling love towards a partner, father, mother, friend, brother or sister. You may feel you want to be with the therapist more and more in the room or even outside of therapy, and ending the session and being without them may be painful. If you recognise these feelings in you, I would say congratulations; they are acceptable, you are not wrong, and these feelings are not something to be ashamed of, in fact, quite the opposite as they have the healing potential within them that may be the most important part of your therapy. These feelings may be healing due to the relevance to your problems, your ability to love, care, and see beauty, and provide a windows into what's missing. I can't stress enough the normalisation and acceptability of these feelings; this happens a fair amount in therapy. In this section, I hope to help you understand these feelings, what you can do with them and how they can be used to accelerate your healing process.

Keywords: Strong feelings that are of a romantic and sexual nature are sometimes called erotic transference.

It must be said at the outset that the relationship between therapist and client can never be more than that. Not only is it unethical for the therapist to engage in anything other than the important therapeutic relationship, it would interfere and be detrimental to helping you in your goals and could result in hurting you more. A therapist is always your therapist only, and that way applies for life (although there may be some exceptions depending on your country or region). However, the good news is that therapists are generally aware of the possibility of this type of attraction and know how to accept and sensitively handle the subject to use it as fuel in aide of your healing.

Warning: *Before making the decision to disclose feelings to your therapist, please reflect on whether your therapist makes you feel safe and secure, keeps boundaries and behaves consistently with you. For example, a therapist who switches between caring, distant, critical or punishing is NOT the therapist to do deep work with on client-therapist attraction, or indeed any therapy.*

There are a number of reasons why disclosure of your feelings, rather than keeping them "below the covers," may be important. Reasons to disclose may be because therapy is stagnating or frozen, your feelings are interfering with the process, and you already feel pain and preoccupations associated with your feelings. There is also a danger that without resolution, therapy will eventually end and you could end up in a worse position than you started, even to the extent of having to spend more time in therapy recovering from this experience.

Regardless of these reasons, you can use therapy to gain a deeper understanding of what these feelings are about, what they mean to you and importantly whether they're related to your problems. You can start by just being curious, accepting and being reflective about them. So, in this context, working through your feelings towards your therapist, either on your own or with the therapist could be a very important part of the work you do. I really recommend you take some steps to work on these feelings; this does not necessarily mean you disclose but it does mean you work on it and make decisions appropriately for your wellbeing. You have four main options: stick with it, disclose, get outside help or move on. The other option of course is to work on these feelings by yourself, reading this section and reflecting and journaling your process using the questions at the end of the section.

Stick with it
If you've just begun therapy and feel the immediate attraction as a distraction, it may subside and you can buckle down without it interfering at all. In this case, your "distraction attraction" will eventually fade into the background, and you can continue without feeling your goals will be impeded. Equally, you may feel the attraction and it does not dissipate, but you may feel you are able to hold the attraction like a separate compartment in a box and thus interfere very little with your therapy. You're able to contain it.

If the feelings are really strong, you may feel not ready, unsure, embarrassed or ashamed of disclosing, which may be a sign that you're just not comfortable yet and the relationship is not strong enough. Part of therapy is about recognizing and respecting your feelings. The decision to stick with it is totally acceptable. You can see how it goes, how your feelings evolve and decide later on whether you want to do anything with those feelings and their relevance to your process.

Disclose to the therapist

If you have built a trusting relationship with your therapist, consider talking about your feelings, especially when they feel intense, reoccurring and distracting. However, I know that disclosure can often be anxiety provoking, but therapists in general are aware of the possibility of client attraction and know how to sensitively handle it to support you in your goals. Although the therapist cannot enter into anything other than a therapeutic relationship, there are a number of reasons in practice why disclosure can be a useful part of the process, lest not because you're already vested in the process; you may have built a good relationship, made progress, and spent time, money and effort in being where you are in therapy.

Here is a non-exhaustive list of potential reasons for disclosure:

- If your process is not moving on or if it is stagnating and you feel the attraction is hurting you or stopping you from making progress.
- It can reveal your missing needs and thus guide you towards a better understanding of yourself. For example, if you have not experienced a warm and safe relationship, the attraction can be identified and explored further.
- Help with patterns of attraction in relationships. You may see similarities of strong feelings with other people or even other therapists, such as unrequited longing or painful rejection that open new paths to explore.
- Uncover how childhood relationships, particularly with caregivers, impacted you in general as well as in adulthood relationships.
- Overcoming your fear, shame and embarrassment of disclosure. Disclosure could alleviate those feelings and help you move forward. Just by disclosure and non-judgmental acceptance by the therapist, you can build confidence in yourself, determine a way forward and relieve the tension. The process can model how shame can be overcome through your courage to be vulnerable.

Because of the dynamic between attraction and rejection, many people find it difficult to make the decision to disclose. These are understandable concerns as you feel the stakes are high when disclosure could lead to loss, rejection, extreme pain and shame. This could in itself be damaging to the extent of having to go into therapy again to overcome the loss. Unfortunately, there are not guarantees whether your therapist will take your disclosure seriously, work with it in depth, or refer you on. I believe most therapists would work on your feelings, but there is no research to back this up. However, in my experience, the following factors, in addition to having already establishing a good relationship, may provide some clues to the therapist's ability to work with your feelings:

- They work for themselves privately. If the therapist works as part of an organization or agency, they may be under outside influence because of internal supervision or policy.
- The therapist has at least five or ten years of experience. It's very unlikely in that time the therapist has not encountered this type of issue directly or raised their own awareness of the possibilities and how best to work with these types of feelings.
- The therapist works psychodynamically/psychoanalytically (insight oriented therapies). These therapists are very likely to be more aware of the possibility and how to work with your feelings. In fact, the term erotic transference comes originally from psychodynamic theory.

Another way of de-risking your concerns is to ask them a few lead-in questions:

"I was reading this book that talks about transference and how past experiences with people can follow you. What do you think about it? Is it real?"

You could even ask, "Do you think it applies to me?"

Another way in is to use feelings you have towards a third party. For example, "I think sometimes that happens to me. I get strong feelings when I like someone a lot and then I get so upset and just think about them so much, and when they leave, it really hurts."

In short, disclosure is an opportunity, maybe the perfect opportunity, because of its intrinsically safe and accepting environment, to gain better understanding of yourself and to take charge of your process.

Consult with an external therapist
If you are unsure of your feelings and need some help to determine what you wish to do, talking to another therapist may be useful. You should see that as therapy coaching rather than your main therapy. Another therapist can provide an opinion, help you understand yourself and help you determine risks to disclosure. A session or two with another therapist maybe useful for coaching you on your process. Another source of external help could be through the country specific regulator or voluntary organizational bodies who may have a helpline for consumers of therapy.

Move on
At any point, you can move on. You may not feel comfortable disclosing, or you may feel that by sticking with it, you're not getting what you need in therapy. Alternatively, if you have already disclosed, you may feel the therapist has not accepted your feelings, did not help you explore it further or even ignored it. It may have driven a wedge in the relationship. In any case, where possible, consider

whether you can talk about how you feel with them; another option could be to call for a review of your therapy with the therapist to see where that leads.

Ultimately, you are free to decide to move on. This shows that you are in touch with your feelings and taking responsibility for your decisions; you are not failing but becoming empowered. If you decide to move on, you can learn about what you need if you move to another therapist. You may learn that you would prefer someone of a different gender. Also remember, you have the option to talk through these feelings at the outset with your new therapist.

Regardless of what you decide to do, don't feel you have to disclose; you are free to choose.

Possible reasons for attraction

- You just are!
- The feelings awaken your dormant child feelings of needing caregivers who were present, attentive, empathic, caring and attuned to your needs.
- They provide a strong emotional crutch, and you feel life would be empty without it.
- The therapist represents a relationship you never had, such as mentor, teacher, family member, or friend.
- You've never really experienced being accepted and cared about.
- Early exposure to sexuality.
- They show your unmet needs as an adult.

Possible reasons to disclose

- The feelings relate to the problems you want to overcome.
- Therapy appears to be stagnating.
- You may already be in emotional pain over your feelings. For example, ending sessions may be difficult and you're preoccupied with the therapist.
- When therapy eventually ends, it may hurt or damage your more.

Possible reasons not to disclose

- You're not ready, or you feel uncomfortable, embarrassed or ashamed.
- You fear you will lose them. They won't accept your feelings or they will "fire you."
- The relationship is not well developed and you feel the therapist will block your feelings rather than work with you in an accepting and non-judgmental manner.

Self-Reflection
When reflecting on your relationship with the therapist, remember it is one-sided;

they are offering undivided caring attention, so there is a natural gap in your understanding of who they are. We all make judgements, and it is possible to imagine personal qualities of the therapist by "filling in the gaps" and imagining how they would be in a relationship. It can in some ways be easier to love someone who spends all their time together completely attending to your feelings without asking anything in return, rather than being in a relationship that is based on balancing two people's needs. Here are some questions for reflection:

What's going on?

1. What are your feelings towards your therapist?
2. What qualities about the therapist appeal to you?
3. How much do you miss or want to be near your therapist when you are or are not with them?
4. Are the feelings intense, persistent, painful, and distracting?
5. How would you label your feelings? For example, one or a combination of emotional, romantic, sexual.
6. Do your feelings resemble particular types of relationships? For example, brotherly, lover, partner, fatherly, sisterly, friendly, teacher or motherly?
7. Are you acting out on your feelings? For example, persistently tracing them on social media, being the "good" client, going out of your way to spot where they are or what they are doing?
8. When did your feelings start to appear? And what was happening? For example, immediately or when you felt more comfortable and shared more?

Understand yourself

9. Does the therapist have any weaknesses or flaws?
10. Have similar feelings occurred with other people or other therapists? Is there an underlying pattern that repeats itself?
11. Did you have caregivers who cared and were empathic and tuned into your needs?
12. Is this the first time you've experienced someone who is totally accepting and is attentive, listening and caring about what you say and about your feelings?
13. Do you struggle with intimacy, or idealizing relationships? Do you control the intimacy where you can keep them at arm's length?
14. Do you find it difficult to love someone with flaws when all is revealed about them? Do you love the idea of the "perfect" partner?
15. How do you prefer relationships to be: mostly focused on them, on you or equal? How does this relate to decisions, intimacy, power, money, love, giving and receiving?

16. Do you want to change anything about your relationships in life? What's missing? Do any of your therapeutic goals relate to relationships, your needs in relationships and what maybe missing?
17. What do you think are the reasons why strong feelings have been evoked?
18. How much do you know about your therapist?
19. What do you imagine they are like outside the room?
20. Is there an element of the unobtainable in your interest? Is the "pining" element of interest to you?
21. Are you fearful or anxious about losing the feelings you have towards your therapist? Why?
22. If you were together outside the room, what would the relationship be like? Imagine it fully. Where would you see it going? What would be happening? Go into lots of detail and write it down. Go into all matters: domestic, intimacy, children, financial, friends, and family. How would the relationship be in 1 month, 3 months, 1 year, and 5 or 10 years' time

What to do

23. Do you feel you are staying with the therapist more because of these feelings rather than your own growth? Or are you conflicted and don't know?
24. Do you feel your feelings for the therapist could interfere and hinder your healing process?
25. Do you want to understand yourself better through the attraction you are feeling?
26. Are you invested in the process? Has it been useful so far? Given your investment of time, effort and money, would it be worth exploring this with your therapist?
27. Do you feel you have a good relationship with the therapist, and have they been accepting, non-judgmental and caring so far? Do you think your therapist would be able to accept your feelings and work with them?
28. Are you fearful of the disclosure? Why?
29. Are you worried the therapist will end your relationship if you disclose? Why?

Summary

- Feelings of attraction and attachment toward the therapist is a known occurrence in therapy.
- Therapists are never allowed to enter into a relationship with you other than a therapeutic one.
- Developing feelings of intense attraction and attachment towards the therapist has healing potential and may be related to your problems.
- These feelings are never wrong or something you need to feel ashamed of.

- These feelings may arise because of your own personal history, particularly your childhood and relationship with caregivers.
- These feelings may block your healing process but if handled well, they may also accelerate it considerably.
- Consider the quality of the relationship before disclosure. Ask whether they accept your feelings, don't judge you, and have consistent boundaries.
- Disclosure has the potential to heal your missing needs.
- Other benefits of disclosure can include alleviation of shame, working to understand your inner child, practicing talking about missing needs, and strengthening your relationship with the therapist.
- If you feel you're in danger of harm because of these feelings, please look after yourself by taking steps that will keep you safe.

Paid to care

In my experience many clients have problems recognising the therapeutic relationship as a caring or meaningful one. Usually it's to do with therapy being their job, money changing hands, the one-way nature of the relationship as well as its well-ordered boundaries.

You may feel the therapist is paid to care, pretends to care, or because they have other clients, you wonder how they could care about you. The truth is, the therapist is usually paid and will most likely have other clients. Ultimately, therapists are human and will have expenses and bills to pay, like most other people.

Here are some examples of the way in which this theme can surface:

- *Client: "I bet you'll be glad to go on holiday; it must get tedious dealing with my issues week after week."*

- *Therapist: "That sounds like a wonderful thing you did by asserting yourself with your friends!" Client: "thanks, I pay you to say that!" [with a smile]*

- *Client: "[directly] you've got other clients, I don't want to know that. I want to make sure I don't see them!"*

One way of reflecting on this concern is based on your own experiences. Are there people you have cared for where you were paid? Is it possible to care for many people simultaneously? Like friends, family, or clients? Can you "fake" care? An oft-quoted phrase in the counselling world is, "You pay me for my time, but my care is free," because you can't force someone to care by paying them; humans simply don't work that way.

If you feel the therapist cares, maybe it is because they do and they have a lot of passion and heart in working with you, so feel free to allow yourself to feel the care. If you have doubts about their care, talk to them and see what comes up. You can use this as a springboard in your healing. Forging a meaningful relationship can be just what you need to heal.

Self-Reflection

1. Does the therapist care? For example, are they working in your interests?
2. What are different types of care?
3. What type of care did you get and would like to have?

Relational cracks

"Tell me if I made a mistake, Tell me if I hurt your feelings, Tell me if there is something missing, Tell me you're not feeling it, Tell me what's working or not, tell me you idealise me, tell me you dislike me. It's all okay."

If you're experiencing safety or even care with your therapist, congratulations; this is the result of the work you have done with the therapist. You have allowed the therapeutic alliance to be built, you should feel proud of this achievement.

However, if there are some relational concerns which are interfering with you feeling safe, or trusting them, you should consider disclosing how you feel to them.

Examples of client's relational concerns

At some stage in the therapy relationship, particularly if it is long-lasting, you are likely to experience some feelings and moments of disappointment, anger, hurt, anxiety, disrespect or other negative emotions towards the therapist, or you may perceive your feelings being minimized. However, as with nearly everything described in this book, nothing is negative in a strategic sense; it's all grist for the mill and an opportunity for you to learn more about yourself as well as build the relationship. Here are feelings I often encounter with people in *therapy coaching*.

- I felt the therapist minimised my feelings by offering suggestions for why I feel this way when all I wanted was to be heard and understood.
- I feel my therapist is not in tune with me and interrupts my train of thought, blocking what I want to talk about.
- My therapist keeps changing the time of my appointments at short notice.
- I found out that my therapist is a trainee and I think she should have told me at the beginning.
- I worry about whether my therapist is good enough.
- My therapist often doesn't say anything and waits for me to speak. The long silences make me feel uncomfortable.
- My therapist used to shake my hand but now doesn't.
- I would feel better if my therapist would give me a hug sometimes, but he won't.
- My therapist said I could message him twice a week but now he's told me to stop.
- I don't understand why my counsellor wants to tape some of my sessions. I don't know if this is normal.
- I feel very uncomfortable because my counsellor takes notes during sessions.
- I read something online about the therapist, and now I can't relax in the same way.
- My therapist is referring me on. I feel she's dumping me and I'm very upset.

- My therapist won't give me any advice although I keep asking her. I expected to be given more help in making decisions.

If you feel something is not right in the relationship, or you're not getting what you need, you have the opportunity to improve it. Even a good therapist can get things wrong and not be aware of it. Equally they can't always know what you're feeling until you tell them. You can take an active part by guarding the relationship, thereby keeping your growth on track. However, if you don't feel safe or ready, that is to be respected too.

Note: Working on relational concerns does not mean accepting unethical or unprofessional practice.

Strategies for exploring your concerns

You have the following options for handling relational concerns you have with the therapist.

First, you can do nothing. Have you ever met someone you didn't immediately like or couldn't get on with? It could be that the relationship is in its very early stages; it will take time to grow and then you can review it later. You can keep it in the back of your mind and see if it clears up.

Second, you can talk to your therapist and let them know what you need to feel safer or to connect better with them. Explaining what you want to improve in the relationship is applicable both inside and outside the therapy room, so it's a useful skill to practice regardless.

A good therapist welcomes you sharing feelings about the relationship, even if you may be critical of them. They know they are not perfect and will want to hear, adjust their approach and talk through it with you. They will want to attune (a fancy word for tuning in or being in tune, like a piano!) to your needs and build the relationship. Your feelings are never wrong and equally they can lead to understanding yourself more, learning to assert your needs and learning how your feelings relate to your experiences in life. This does not mean the therapist won't give their perspective, but they do so in the interests of furthering your process.

Here are some examples of how you can broach this:

"There was something I wanted to talk to you about, but I am a bit nervous of your reaction. Whenever I get into the flow of things, I feel interrupted and what you're saying feels kind of out of tune with what I want to explore. I appreciate you trying to do the best for me, but I just need a bit more space in my mind."

"You said that I am creating a lot of distance in relationships and acting in a way that pushes people away, but when you said it, I perceived my feelings being minimised and I was hurt."

Improving the relationship may also help your healing:

"That was the milestone event for me: asking for what I needed from the therapist. The therapist really cared about my feelings and admitted they did not realise that was something I needed help with. I realised deep down that I can't really expect people to know what I need, so taking responsibility was really empowering. Last night I was sitting in bed with my partner and thinking she must really not like me at the moment because I'm out of work, and she has had to take on more work. I was really getting low about it. I asked her, and she did have concerns about us being able to cope financially, but she assured me she didn't blame me for it. We're getting along a bit better because of it."

Talking about your feelings about the relationship is not always easy, especially if you're not used to asserting yourself and are nervous about their reaction, for example, feeling fearful of being criticised by the therapist. Even if you're tentative, here are a few ways you may feel safer to segue into talking about your needs in the relationship.

"I really find it hard to express what's wrong sometimes. Can you help me with that?" It may be possible through this dialogue to see if you're ready to share feelings about the therapeutic relationship too.

Ask for a review: "Can we review my progress and what I could work on?"

If you're struggling to share something important you could also consider secure message, email or write what you feel in a diary to read to the therapist.

The third option is, of course, to consider leaving the therapist. You may not be ready to talk about your feelings and needs, or you may not trust the therapist to respond well (a therapist should not be critical of you or blame you). Respecting your feelings is important too: if, at that point, you feel the therapist is not right for you, then that is your truth.

Working with therapy coaching clients, I have to be realistic that there is always a possibility the therapist will not react with care. If this has happened to you, for example, minimising your feelings or not listening to them, then you can try and resolve the conflict if you wish, but you have to decide whether it's worthwhile continuing, especially if the feelings are left unresolved and you no longer feel safe to be yourself in therapy. A more likely philosophical attitude would be something like this:

"Well, I tried and I felt really hurt by the therapist that he did not acknowledge my feelings. I know I said it when I was a bit angry, but that's no excuse. After all, I am there to get help. Well, if he was like that, he can't be right for me, and this saves me a lot of time and money. It was just not working for me. I'll bring this up with my next therapist. I hope they can tolerate some feedback."

If you've given it your best shot and asked for help, but it's still not working for you, you should consider leaving because you have done your fair share in building the relationship. There is little point staying if you've come to a cul-de-sac, taken the time and made the effort to make things work better, but it is still not working. Remember you do still have the option to explore what happened with your next therapist. If such an exchange has left you with emotional wounds, please consider seeking support.

Self-Reflection

1. Do you feel your therapist is competent? Why?
2. Does the therapeutic relationship mean something to you?
3. Do you tell people when they have said something that annoys, frustrates, angers or makes you sad?
4. Do you understand why you do, or do not share your feelings? Will you share in certain settings or with certain people more?
5. Are you afraid of sharing your feelings with the therapist? What do you imagine the consequences of doing so would be?
6. Are there moments with the therapist where you felt discomfort, irritation or wished for a different response? Write about why that is.
7. Is there anything you could do to strengthen the relationship?
8. Do you believe the therapist is accepting, caring or empathic?
9. Is there anything missing in the relationship which would help you?

This isn't working

In reading this section, perspectives in favour of having an ending time with the therapist are given. However, you should only do this if you're ready, feel safe and importantly, if you wish to. You are free to choose how to end.

When you initiate an ending with unresolved problems, unless it will cause harm or you're not ready, regardless of the reason for leaving, always work through your feelings, thoughts and decision process with the therapist first.

In this way you will learn about the potential upsides of talking to the therapist whenever you wish to initiate an ending, especially prior to leaving with unresolved concerns. In particular, you will understand how conflicts (sometimes called rupture and repair) in the relationship can—if handled well by both you and the therapist—be of enormous therapeutic value.

You may decide to leave therapy for any number of reasons including:

- You feel worse.
- You're not ready or therapy is not for you.
- You feel the therapist may be thinking badly of you.
- You don't want to be rejected by the therapist, so want to end it first
- You feel you don't deserve to be in therapy any longer.
- You don't feel connected to the therapist.
- There is something intangible you don't like about the therapist.
- You're not improving.
- Your ideal in how you envisaged the therapist and the process to be has not been met.
- You come into contact with new memories and thoughts which you are aren't ready to bring into awareness.
- You don't feel therapy is going to work for you.
- The pace of therapy is too fast or too slow.
- The therapist said or did something you didn't like.
- The process of therapy feels threatening. For example, going to your inner feelings and experiences.
- Life priorities and money.

The objective in talking about your reasons to end is, of course, to learn something new. By exploring the end you can check out your feelings, see if the relationship can be repaired, check out the therapist's perspective, learn a new way to deal with feelings including endings, and determine whether there is therapeutic value in exploring your reasons.

Talking to the therapist does not take away your decision and your freedom to choose. For example, the therapist may not be right for you or you may feel that their way of working is not suited to you. But by checking out your feelings, it could provide closure or even accelerate your process. If this doesn't yield any benefits you have still learnt to speak about your feelings, and you can end gracefully. If a therapist is critical or does not accept your feelings it obviously confirms your decision to leave, so in that sense even a negative experience can be seen as an acknowledgement that your feelings are in harmony with reality.

Rupture and repair

Rupture is a term in therapy used to describe the underlying strain or breakdown in the relationship between you and the therapist. For the purposes of this section, I extend the definition to include a rupture between you and therapy, which is a felt internal threat from acknowledging your own feelings to yourself and the therapist.

In moments of rupture you can feel threatened by what the therapist does or says, or by the challenge of the therapy process. Ruptures may sit silent and unsaid, or they can burst out in the room through anger. They may even result in you walking out of the room. These ruptures are common in therapy and good therapists know how to work with you when they occur, because they know it can be a breakthrough moment in therapy.

Therapy, by nature, can be a challenging encounter even if you feel comfortable talking about yourself. There is a part of you which you have learnt to keep hidden, sometimes even from yourself, and this can be loosely referred to as the "inner child", which is a symbol of your most important early development in life. This part can feel threatened by the experience of therapy for a wide range of reasons, which you may not even be aware of:

- Feeling less powerful than the therapist. For example, less competent, or you feel they are viewing you through a critical or analytical gaze.
- Vulnerability. The inner part of you is threatened because it is never shown to anyone, let alone a stranger. Your internal parts feel under threat of shame at the thought of being revealed in the room.
- The therapist may say something that pushes a button in you. For example, being belittled, not believed, judged, challenged or put under pressure.
- Due to an injustice. This can come up if you believe the therapist is not being fair or sensitive.
- Loss of control. Experiencing feelings where you say or do something that you regret. You feel you made a mistake and say something you feel you should not have said, either about yourself or the therapist.

- A way of relating. For example, you become uncomfortable when the relationship with the therapist becomes closer. You feel exposed or are fearful that once you reveal the "authentic you" you will be abandoned or rejected. There is part of you that does not feel good enough in the relationship.

These threats can trigger in you the need to take control and power back from the encounter; this may be through abruptly leaving session, ghosting the therapist or even harshly challenging them. Here are some examples of the inner narrative of clients seeking to take control back from the encounter of therapy.

Tim was really silent in therapy. The therapist was tentative in the session; he did not want to rush his client, but he was not attuned to the fact that his client felt really uncomfortable with the long pauses. The client left feedback later by email that the therapist had "freaked him out" by being too silent. Tim did not return to therapy.

David had cancelled sessions outside the 24 hour time limit. On the second occasion, the therapist reminded the client this had happened a few times. However, the client felt a sense of judgement and criticism, even though the therapist was highlighting boundaries. He never returned any messages and terminated three months of therapy.

Tina was feeling increasingly tentative about therapy; as she started to talk more about feelings about her partner and her relationship, the therapist noticed how her breathing would change, words would become slower and she would put a lid on it quickly with phrases like "Relationships are not easy." She decided to end therapy by sending in an email after the session.

In all these cases, these clients did the right thing, which is employing their right to choose. But therapists can make mistakes, and try as they may to reduce the possibilities of rupture, they won't always be able to meet your needs because they can't know everything. In Tina's case she was clearly not ready to admit, perhaps even to herself her feelings about her relationship.

After a sudden relational rupture, it is possible that you will end the session immediately, and not return because you feel aggrieved, or because you feel embarrassed by your actions. However, a good therapist will accept your feelings and work with them, and while they may express their own thoughts, including their boundaries, they are there to work in your best interests. Working through the impasse could be the most liberating part of therapy.

Another reason for ending without talking to the therapist is that therapy may be making you feel worse. Therapy is not always a straight line, nor is it a process without difficulties, so you may feel worse before feeling better. Feeling worse in therapy can appear to be self-defeating or hopeless, when in fact, it could be the opposite. For example, you may be edging towards facing feelings you are unaware of or mourning a loss. However, just because you're feeling worse, or if more pain is being experienced, that does not imply that it's healthy either. Talk to your therapist and/or physician if you have concerns about feeling worse.

Therapy is an opportunity to explore, perhaps for the first time, to check out your feelings and assumptions, by telling the therapist what you need or what is missing. Of course, none of this is guaranteed to repair the relationship or lead to further insights, but on the other hand, it may be the most important catalyst for recovery.

So if you are ready and it's safe, don't walk away until you have said what you feel and why you want to leave. Take a risk and say what you don't like, even if you don't know exactly why. Sticking around during the difficult periods to explore reasons for ending—even over a number of sessions—could be just what is needed to take your process to the next level.

Self-Reflection

1. How do you normally deal with conflict whether it's with friends, family or at work?
2. Have you sometimes felt, even temporarily, that you wanted to leave therapy? Is that something you can talk to the therapist about?
3. Have you had doubts whether therapy is going to work for you? Is that something you can talk to the therapist about?
4. Do you have any anxieties, fears or feelings in talking about your reasons for initiating the ending? Is that something you can talk to the therapist about?
5. Have you ever wanted to "get away" because you felt trapped or thought people won't listen or understand without saying why?
6. Are you concerned about feeling less competent, "smaller" or less powerful in the therapeutic encounter?
7. Are you concerned about "being seen" in therapy by the therapist as you are, "warts and all"?
8. What do you think you won't like in therapy or about the therapist that would "turn you off" being in therapy? Can you share that with the therapist?

Chapter 3 – Themes of surfacing beliefs

What do you feel about being there in therapy and having the focus of the therapist's attention on you? Maybe you believe you need to be "good", that you're "wasting the therapists time" or perhaps you believe "it's wrong to feel". These beliefs could can bring to the surface what you believe about yourself and your world, and thus be of therapeutic value in your process.

In this chapter, I explore perhaps the most frequently occurring beliefs that surface as a result of the therapeutic experience. As with all the themes in this book, not all will be applicable to you, but if any resonate, then that is a good opportunity for further self-reflection and potential work with the therapist.

I'm wasting your time

Are these words familiar? "I feel bad because others could be getting help," "I'm wasting your time" or "I'm sure you've got other people to see." What is behind the words? These statements can also be a window into what people may think about themselves and in comparison to other people in the world.

These feelings may arise because you feel stuck, don't know what to say or feel you must perform for the therapist, to be good at it. You feel you fall below importance or expectation; therefore, you are wasting your time as well as the therapist's time. The feeling of "not performing to expectations" may be an intrinsic part of the overarching therapy process of how you feel in yourself. However, the therapist is not there to judge you, but to accept you (See "Be me?").

Here are some possible reasons you may feel "you're wasting the therapist's time." If any resonate, you can explore them in therapy:

- You feel you are not being productive in therapy, but you need to be, so you are wasting the therapist's time.
- You value yourself less than others.
- You were not given a sense of worth during childhood.
- You want to be compared with others and thus seen as "normal."
- A perception that clients come with very disturbing issues but you don't (See "Others suffer more").
- What you're saying is trivial to the therapist. If it's not important to them, you're not important. Were you important growing up?
- You don't feel the therapist does or could care because you do not have problems like others. They will only care if someone has a perceived bigger issue.
- You don't feel good about yourself and never got a lot of attention and care; ultimately, you don't deserve people's time and care (See "Don't be").

Self-Reflection

1. Have you ever found yourself in therapy or outside of therapy saying in your mind or out loud, "I shouldn't take up your time," "Sorry to take up your time," or "I'm sure you've got better things to do." What do you think it means?
2. How are you in relationships, in work and in general with receiving care? Do you feel bad talking and taking up people's time? Do you share yourself more, listen more or a mixture? Is your role that of a helper of others?

Be good

Therapy may also make you feel that you have to perform well, like a "good client," or that you must know the answers. You may feel internal pressure to perform, or to meet the therapist's expectations as well as ultimately to achieve a good outcome. On the other hand, part of this may have to do with being vulnerable, having difficulty asking for help, feeling less power or feeling you need to be competent and good at therapy. The consequence to the process of being "good" could actually be detrimental to your process, because it's the equivalent of wearing a false mask, showing a side of you. However, as therapy is about the whole of you, the more you reveal all parts of you, the more you can work on the truth behind the mask. In therapy, try your best to be yourself, and even if you don't know to be the "whole of you" in the room, simply saying that you're not sure who you are can be best you can do.

Therapy may make you feel an internal pressure to perform well. But therapy isn't an exam or an interview where your performance will be judged. If you try to perform well by saying or doing what you think the therapist requires from you, then it could hinder your process.

Being "a good client" is the equivalent of wearing a mask, showing a side of you, while hiding others. For example, if you feel a need to please the therapist for fear they will "dump" you, it is easy to see how it will hide the vulnerable parts of you that you're fearful of showing. It may have to do with being vulnerable, having difficulty asking for help, feeling less power or feeling you need to be competent and good at therapy. The consequence to the process of being "good" could actually be detrimental to your process, because it's the equivalent of wearing a false mask, showing one side of you. However, as therapy is about the whole of you, the more you reveal all parts of you, including wanting to be "good" the more you can illuminate about yourself.

If you have become aware of feeling you need to be a good client, then it's an opportunity to explore in therapy. You can reflect on what the need is to be seen as "good", and see if it links to your difficulties. Usually, at the heart of this need lies fear, the fear of being seen as you are, being judged or rejected. Of course, therapy relies on your engagement to want to work on yourself, but therapy does not intrinsically require a particular standard or ideal for you to satisfy your role. It's about working with you as you are, including wanting to be a good client. If you're busy trying to be good, then try to be the bad client.

Self-reflection

1. Do you feel a need to please the therapist?
2. In what situations in your history have you had to please people, and why?
3. What were the benefits of being good and pleasing others?
4. What are the downsides of being the "good client" or pleasing others?
5. Are there parts of you that would seem "bad" or "unacceptable" if you were to take down the "good client" mask? Which parts?

Be self-sufficient

Mark was a hypnotherapist by trade. He entered therapy wanting help with his depression. He would come into therapy committed and regular. He would often look away when talking to the therapist showing little "relational presence." He would try and find answers himself by answering the questions analytically, like a forensics investigator. He always seemed to take suggestions on board that were offered but the therapist felt for some reason, he was "not being allowed to help." He understood that this may be an assumption and decided to check it out with Mark.

Therapist: Mark, sometimes I feel when you're talking, I am kept out. I don't know if that is something that resonates with you?

Mark: [Pauses.] I don't know what that is... err...I don't know.

Therapist: Well, I want you to know that I am here in this room with what you are saying.

Mark: Thanks. I usually do talk a lot... almost as if I'm talking to myself most of the time. I am so used to being the one giving help. I don't usually ask for it, and I feel really uncomfortable. My body tenses up when I receive help.

Therapist: Ah, right.. How does that work between us?

Mark: [Pauses.] When I think about it more, I would say I do feel tension when you offer a suggestion. I feel anxious..

This excerpt shows the opening of a door into felt experiences Mark has around being helped and self-sufficient, which of course may link aspects of his problems.

The therapist is there to help you; you don't need to do this alone.

Self-Reflection

1.   Are you self-sufficient? If so, how and why?
2.   Do you prefer to work on tasks as an individual or in a group?
3.   Do you like to share your expertise, likes, dislikes, feelings and knowledge?

What do you imagine it's like to be courageous? Perhaps you think of fighting in a war, a parachute jump, or public speaking. These are all very courageous activities, particularly if those things scare you, but there is another type of courage that is internal: that of overcoming an internal struggle to be able to reveal and talk about parts of yourself that you find difficult or even shameful to explore. These parts may represent behaviors, memories or what you believe about yourself; they are typically deeper feelings. You may find it hard to talk about having an affair, spending time in prison, feeling guilty for being a "bad" daughter, being envious or of having obsessional thoughts. Courage of this sort, if you're ready, is the inner courage of the heart, to allow the authentic parts of you to finally breathe and be allowed into existence. It can be the key to unlocking your process of healing.

Parts can remain hidden from you and from others because of fears of their acceptability if exposed, even to yourself. For example, you may have developed a protective wall to keep people away from your personal life because you experienced personal matters being continually being used against you; so to fit in, you've given up revealing any of your personal life, even what you did at the weekend, or your hobbies. You can call this the "suspicious" part of you. But you have to ask how this serving you now. This wall may have been useful in stopping further hurt at the time, but is it useful that you're hiding so much of yourself, including from friends and family?

Here are a few examples of how vulnerability may sound like in the room. The first example is a way of moving away from being vulnerable and delving too far into your actual hurt; instead, you seek to focus in on "wishing the feeling away" by trying to find logical solutions to fix the feelings:

"My mind is so irrational. I get angry so quickly when someone does not include me or ask me a question or ask me how I am. I lash out in anger and it takes me a while to recover. I feel bad that I get angry, so I end up apologising. This pushes people away so I just need to think differently. It's no one else's responsibility to care about me, it's not good, and my reactions are over the top. I am listening to a lot of meditation exercises just to balance myself."

In the second example, a client is allowing himself to be vulnerable by exploring how he really feels deep inside when anger appears:

"There is something I wanted to talk to you about for a while. I just find it really difficult to say because it feels so irrational and not normal. You know when I was saying I felt hurt when my friend does not seem to care about me? It reminds me of how... well, of how I have never—I can't believe I'm saying this out loud—truly been

part of anything. I don't feel heard, and I just feel invisible all the time. I was controlled by my family and the church, and I was never allowed opinions. I just didn't matter to anyone. No one accepted me and I was bullied at school for years. I try and I try, but deep down, it feels that people see something defective in me, inferior or not worth it. I just end up being a listener but it hurts real badly because no one seems to care about me. It's almost as if I don't exist."

Sometimes, you may find revealing anything about yourself can be so deeply entrenched, that even if you wanted to share more, you cannot, it's as though you are fighting your mind and body which has other ideas about you even attempting to share.

Julie explained how it felt to her any time she had to confront her feelings. First, a strong feeling would appear in her gut. It felt scary, like a numbness. It felt so overwhelming that her mind would go blank and then she felt that she had to escape the situation and distract herself by doing something different. She said she tried to stay with the feelings but her mind would shut down on her behalf.

Being vulnerable is showing up, facing the feelings and fears, letting go of inner protections, allowing yourself to be free, and showing your human fragility. This, in itself, can be a powerful therapeutic agent for change.

Self-reflection (vulnerability)

1. When was the last time you felt vulnerable?
2. When was the last time you were vulnerable in front of others? What happened?
3. How does vulnerability feel for you? How vulnerable do you allow yourself to be?
4. When are you the most vulnerable?
5. Are you feeling okay about being vulnerable or do you feel a bit scared?
6. Would you like to be more vulnerable in therapy or within relationships? If so, in what way?
7. Are there things you feel ashamed about? That you would not want to disclose to the therapist? Why? Are they related to your goals?
8. Do you need help being vulnerable? Can you broach being more vulnerable by just talking about your feelings of vulnerability with the therapist?
9. If you want to work on vulnerability, develop a hierarchy of vulnerability. Draw up a list of vulnerability tasks based on easiest to worst so you can practice vulnerability. For example, an easier task may be sharing that you found something difficult, while a more challenging one could be sharing what you don't like about your body.

10. What is the worst that could happen if you were vulnerable with the therapist? Or with others?
11. Do you feel ashamed that you are fearful of being vulnerable? That's okay; take it in small doses or stages. You may not need or be ready to be more vulnerable until you feel safe enough with the therapist.

"You say your feelings are wrong, first look for reasons why they may be right"

Your feelings are never wrong from a therapeutic perspective, just like the readings on a car dashboard are never wrong (well, rarely!). If the engine is overheating, it tells you to do something about it, otherwise the car may break down. Similarly, feelings are indicators that something needs attention before change can happen, whether it's a tweak, a significant overhaul or something you need. Acknowledging feelings doesn't mean you don't want to change; it points you to the change needed for your wellbeing. Feelings are to be respected for what they are and explored as windows into what is going on, and when you have worked them out or *processed* them, change is possible.

Ignoring feelings can be like changing the lightbulbs when the engine needs fixing. Similarly, if there is a mismatch between the sources of feeling(s) and solution(s) to your problem(s), you could end up working on something that is less relevant in the hope you'll strike gold.

Remember, respecting feelings or allowing feelings is a process. It does not mean you will be able to do that immediately. For example, if your feelings have been dampened down, getting in touch with them can take time. Similarly, feelings don't always have to be explored, you're free to choose.

What do we mean by processing feelings? Processing feelings means to become aware of them, understand them, to gain perspective(s) of them or even experience them bodily so they can be healed. A metaphor of healing taking the plaster off a wound, caring for it, letting it air, bandaging it up, and allowing it time to heal.

Bypassing feelings

A common pattern in therapy is to dismiss feelings as wrong, unacceptable or scary, which results in leaving the feelings unprocessed and unresolved. However, instead of rejecting or criticising your feelings, therapy allows you to process them and— when appropriate, to use and convert these feelings over time. As an example, therapy does not generally look at feelings such as anger and try to manage them away, although that may help. For deeper issues, their root(s) would need to be understood to heal its source. Feelings can be embraced and understood in therapy.

A narrative of ignoring or pushing past strong deep-rooted feelings may sound something like this:

Paul: "You know, I really felt hurt by my friends [eyes tearing up] over the weekend. I don't know what it is about me, that I feel people ignore me and my feelings. This happens a lot; it hurts, but I have to get over it, think more positively and not depend on people to meet my needs or get so attached to them."

Therapist: "I can see you are hurting underneath [long pause]. You're really trying to push through and think positively. You can do that but I'd really like to understand the part of you that felt angry and sad for being left out."

It's tempting, especially when you feel strong feelings, to rationalise them or "fix" them away, but if you feel something, you feel it! Ignoring those feelings would be equivalent to ignoring a child's feeling and saying, "Don't be silly, just grow up!" That is not to say that rationality is not important or challenging—whether there is evidence for feeling the way you do or not; it may be a very important part of this solution but give feelings enough airtime first. Allow understanding, nurturing, self-care and even love to be provided to the feeling parts of you.

Respecting your feelings is a core part of caring for your wounds.

Dampened Feelings
"Gurnal was very agreeable, he liked to be liked, hated being judged and never got into conflicts. Only the fantasy bubble of being "good" had just been broken as he sat opposite me full of anxiety and hurt. He had come to realise his wife had controlled every aspect of his life: from what he should wear and eat, to who he should meet. He had become isolated from friends and family because his partner did not like them. He now asked "Where was I all this time? It's like I lost myself but I don't know who 'myself' is!"

For some, feelings may be so dampened down, that you don't trust your feelings, or that you emphasise others' feelings more—including the therapist's—more than your own. This may be because you believe others know best, so you don't listen to your own feelings. You may "give in" to others because you feel you are wrong, or because you don't see the point since others don't listen. If you realise that you tend to quieten or damp down your own feelings then I recommend exploring this further and bringing it up with your therapist.

Sometimes your feelings may be hidden so far deep inside you they that it will take much work before they come to the fore. Feelings may arise which were previously unsighted, sometimes at the peak point of your change process. Although this may not happen for you, the distancing and dampening down of feelings can occur over a long period of time, as a way of coping or even surviving in life. The feelings become like a dormant volcano. Examples of dormant feelings may include a bereavement, a trauma, or even a painful memory; all forgotten but sat within the body and mind, like an old unattended wound.

Dampening down your feelings can have consequences in the therapeutic process too, such as stagnation in therapy, not being able to share difficult feelings or remaining with a therapist who is not right you.

Having feelings may be overwhelming in therapy so it is important to feel safe. For highly distressing or very low feelings this could mean staying somewhere in the middle between having feelings and being present with the therapist in order to process them. Speak to your therapist if you have concerns about triggering strong feelings, remembering that strongly felt feelings could be a much-needed part of your process.

Finding the source(s) of your feelings

It may also be difficult to allow or explore feelings because there does not appear to be a reason for them. This can confuse both you and those around you.

As your feelings are triggered, you could get caught up in them and instead of owning them, you end up protecting yourself from them by blaming yourself or others as a way of coping with the confusion. Creating mental space to look below the surface and gain an understanding of these emotions, particularly when things have cooled down, is often needed.

Stephen had a huge release of anger a few weeks back. He had been tidying up some of his wife's bathroom items; they had both been meaning to get around it. However, when his wife returned, she told him that he should not have moved her things and she "would have eventually cleaned up." At that point Stephen, very unusually for him, went into a rage. He was very surprised, and so was his partner.

After much exploration of his feelings, he uncovered many factors that led up to that point. He came to realise how he tried to contain his feelings, rather than take steps to work through them. In particular, he felt his partner had not listened to him for a number of years, and he could not understand why she could not think like him too. Then there was his own history of not sharing feelings, being dissatisfied at work and feeling anxious about the future. He found some of these feelings related to unresolved feelings from his past, in particular how his family never kept a financial safety net, which made him worry they would be kicked out of their home.

The anger expressed towards his wife gave him a window to explore what lay beneath the emotions, rather than go straight to a logical solution which assumed feeling had to be fixed rather than being heard. This example also shows how feelings and reactions can have many strands that can appear to be unrelated to symptoms but are more about discovering and processing frustrations that have not yet been aired.

You may not know why you are feeling a certain way, but by giving your feelings time and space, you'll pick up some possibilities as your process unfolds. It is pretty rare to not find some possible reasons for feeling a certain way.

Getting to feelings

Deeper feelings aren't something you can directly pull out of the bag. In fact, if you make it an objective to get to your feelings it often becomes more elusive. Rather, getting to your feelings—especially if you're unaware of them or they lie dormant—can come about spontaneously or gradually during the process. Mostly, all you can do is to freely explore your experiences and let the relational container of therapy do its job.

You can start using the language of feelings when expressing your experiences. Here are some ways to describe feelings:

- Label your feelings. For example, jealousy, anger, emptiness, excitement and rage.
- Describe the feeling as a picture or image. For example, confusion may be expressed as mist and hopelessness could be described as being in a dark well.
- Describe where a feeling is in the body: its colour, texture, shape, temperature and intensity.
- Associate feelings with memories and events in which you had similar feelings.
- Using metaphors, stories or myths which represent your feelings

You can also observe any language you use which minimises feelings. Of course many of these are feeling-based and can be explored too:

- I'm not normal or I'm crazy
- Others have it worse
- It's not their fault
- I'm to blame for how I feel
- Self-criticism. For example, I never get it right or I shouldn't feel this way.

You can also familiarise yourself with the various forms in which feelings can be expressed:

- By using "I feel..." or "I felt.." statements.
- As live bodily felt sensations.
- As a lack of feeling sometimes called emptiness or numbness.
- As feelings which you quickly close off as being difficult, shameful or wrong.
- A mismatch between what you say and how your body expresses itself. For example, talking about difficult experiences and smiling or laughing over them (minimised feelings).
- Silence.

You can also observe and reflect on whether you are keeping a distance from your feelings through your awareness of them).

Learning to acknowledge more of your feelings can be a difficult path, especially if have come from an environment or family where feelings were not shown or allowed. You may also feel guilt or shame for talking about feelings out of a sense of disloyalty, or even fear of consequences. In other cases it may be that you have an inbuilt way of shutting down feelings through self-criticism, believing no one is interested, which causes you to believe that feelings are "abnormal". So allow your feelings to surface in stages and work on what interferes with their expression. Of course, this does not mean you should share feelings if you are not ready, but if you are and you feel it's important, then take steps.

If you have difficulty talking about feelings here are some strategies:

- Tell the therapist that you have difficulties talking about your feelings. Therapists usually have many methods to help you.
- Talk about any obstacles that stop you talking about feelings. For example, feeling that you would be betraying someone if you shared what you really felt.
- Talk about your historical experiences of showing feelings when growing up.
- Use awareness to determine whether you are minimising or criticising your feelings inadvertently.

Where possible don't shut feelings out of therapy—even if you don't like them, are confused by them, feel ashamed, self-critical or feel they are irrational—until they are understood. Your own subjective feelings are going to be an important source of the work you do in therapy.

Allowing feelings does not mean that you don't stand back and check out their truth, you will in time, and that can be important too. But unless there is a safety concern, allow your feelings to breathe, because allowing them to be expressed, processed or felt in the room is a big part of what makes therapy work.

Self-Reflection

1. What are your beliefs about feelings? Do you, your family and friends show feelings?
2. What is your approach to expressing feelings?
3. What is your family's approach to expressing feelings?
4. Do you generally try and figure out why you may be feeling a certain way? For example, happy, energised, excited, sad, emotional, angry, low, numb?
5. Do you believe your feelings are balanced and in accord with the trigger that made you feel something?

6. Have you ever felt emotions without understanding why it was happening or what was causing it? For example, anxious, feeling low, emotional, and angry.
    a. Does your lack of emotion or high intensity of emotion sometimes surprise you?
    b. Do you have some examples where you felt unexpected emotions? Trace back from that time and write about what was happening five days before the situation and whether there were any stresses or triggers. Remember, stresses may be a lack of a need, e.g., feeling lonely.
    c. How long has this been happening? If this has been happening for a long time what factors do you believe contributed to your current feelings? Consider writing your life story to see if it reveals any new ideas.
    d. If you can't figure it out by yourself, try and ask others whom you trust and know.
7. Do you share feelings in therapy? Are there feelings you want to share but are not ready to do so?
8. Are there any feelings or beliefs which inhibit you from sharing more of your feelings?
9. Do you want to share more feelings? If so, develop your own personalised hierarchy of difficulty for sharing feelings.

Lost self

Socrates was on trial and accused of blasphemy against the gods, inventing new deities and corrupting the youth. The accusers gave such a powerful and moving account of why Socrates should be found guilty. After the end of the accuser's rhetoric, Socrates took a lengthy pause and said:

"I do not know, men of Athens, how my accusers affected you; as for me, I was almost carried away in spite of myself, so persuasively did they speak. And yet, hardly anything of what they said is true."

Socrates was clearly entranced by the mesmerising account of his misdeeds that even the wise Socrates was taken in; he lost himself and almost believed what the accusers had said was true. He had to get back into his own mind and to his own internal frame of reference to understand that hardly anything said was really true.

This is something that you may also discover in therapy, that aspects of you are lost in the world, outside yourself. Often others become central, and the external world is where you focus your mind more. Whether it's your beliefs, who you are, what to do, decisions, and self-care, they are externally determined rather than by you in relation to the world.

Lucy had spent most of her life caring for others. She was the eldest of three children. She had been a carer for her mother when she was being beaten by her dad and also had to fill in to care for her siblings. Her father and mother also controlled her and her decisions, because she was not able to do things "like other children." This became her norm to care for others and to need her parents to tell her what to do in life. As a grownup, she sought relationships where she could continue that role and was particularly attracted to ambitious and "righteous" men, who knew how the world worked and what to do. She continued to "go along" with others who understood the world more and she wanted to care for people even though she did not feel cared for by her family or partner. She spent twenty years of marriage in state of being entranced by people and the world. She entered therapy because she had reached a stage where she could not do it anymore, and she did not want to be invisible anymore. She had lost herself and wanted to return to her own mind.

If parts of this resonate for you, you can ask at what expense and whether the way of being is what you want now. This is not to say that continuously caring for others is not the right path, it means that you recognise the impact to you. Communities, relationships, family and groups thrive based on reciprocity, which means you give and you receive. However, if you are the end of the chain and no one is particularly "giving" or championing you, you can feel as if you have dropped off the edge. Therapy is an opportunity to put yourself in centre stage, to see the world in relation to you. This is what "finding yourself" can mean.

What do I need?

Exploring what you need now can often lead to understand more about what's missing in your life. Psychological needs are an extension of our basic survival needs, such as food, warmth, and shelter. Often, in the process of therapy, you'll ask, "What do I need?" or even, "What don't I need?" Your needs, both in life and in therapy, may come to the fore at different stages, and usually the more you come in touch with your truth of what is wrong, deficits in your needs become conscious to you.

Here is a narrative of someone approaching their own needs in life:

Gerry understood the deeper hurt he felt towards his mum:

"I've had enough of this; she has caused me and my family so much hurt over the years. I know she has an illness, but everyone gave everything. She could at least care about me and what I'm going through. She's always thinking of herself. She keeps hurting me!"

Then he became more aware of his needs and of how to attend to them:

"What about me? I am neglecting my own family and kids and even myself. Everyone's life is put first except mine. I need do what I want to do more, to spend more time with my family."

Gerry decided to focus more on meeting his own needs by living life so that he was doing what he wanted to do and develop deeper relationships with his own family, rather than spending so much time on seeking unobtainable closeness with his mum. His mum was not in a position to give that. He still supported his mum but no longer was tied to the wish that she could be the "mum" he wanted.

It is not uncommon to feel out of touch with your needs, especially at the start of therapy; however, once you get in touch with your feelings and you gain clarity and awareness about your life, you may come to understand what you need more and more. Keep asking, *what do I need?* Whether it's a life purpose, a caring relationship, life projects, or better friends, needs are a source of nutrition for well-being.

Self-Reflection

1. What needs were missing in my childhood?
2. Do you have the relationships you want with caregivers, family, and friends? Are your needs met? If not, can they be improved or do they need to be obtained somewhere else?
3. Do you want a life project or a task to pursue?
4. Do you feel a sense of belonging in your family and in your community?
5. Do you feel you give more than you receive? Is that an issue?

6. What needs are missing in your life? How do these relate to your childhood?

Note that needs may include privacy, community, love, work, life projects, passions, and/or relationships.

7. How can you get your needs met, e.g., share more or ask for it?
8. What are the obstacles to getting your needs met?
9. How much of what you do, understand or believe comes from your own understanding rather than people and the world?

Others suffer more

A common theme that can come up in therapy is a feeling that you including your therapy is less important than others because others have it worse. This may be a deep-rooted feeling of not being important, no one wants to understand or you have the role of being the helper, where you help others but have not had or want the help yourself. This type of feeling, particularly if it is deep-rooted, is something you may need to understand more as a natural part of the therapeutic process.

However, what do we do with that feeling to make it okay, or at least to get you going on the process, even if it is looking at it from a more rational perspective? Well, first I would say that we all suffer and go through hardship in life; no one is completely isolated or immune to be on the receiving end of suffering – whether its bereavement, an illness, a relationship breakup or a trauma. We will, and likely have, already suffered hardships in life.

Second, suffering is relative. At different points in time, depending on conditions and opportunity, there are always people who are suffering more or less than you. If this was done scientifically to measure, where would you really be? I suspect if you are in therapy, you will experience suffering by nature of the process. Ask "Would people suffering less than you be deserving of help and understanding?"

The third point is that if you feel better in yourself, it will have a positive effect on others, such as your family, children, friends, community or co-workers. Think about whether you feeling better would help others? For example, would it cause you to be closer with a partner, or for your children to enjoy time with you more? Prioritising you and whatever is causing your problems can be beneficial to you and to others around you.

From a therapist's perspective, you are naturally in sessions with them and will be an important priority to them, so really explore how that feels, what makes you feel that way and whether it would be okay for you to be prioritised and helped in therapy. Share what it is like to be prioritised. The feelings around it may be directly linked to the problems you are experiencing.

Self-Reflection

1. Do you feel you should not be getting help in therapy because others have it worse?
2. What would you say if it was a loved one in a similar position to you? Would it still be the same response?
3. Do you feel the therapist is good enough to be allowed to care or help?

4. What are the reasons for this feeling? For example, think about how you get your needs met.
5. What benefits would feeling better have on yourself and others?
6. Are there people who suffer less than you? Would they be deserving of help that would cause them to get better?

Labels are really useful in life. They help us identify things and what they mean. Without labels, we would have no idea what town we lived in, what food we were buying or what the term "bachelor" means. However, when it comes to labels to define who you are, your problems, and your emotional world, things get more complicated. When we label ourselves in therapy with an assumed or an official mental health diagnosis, it can have the inadvertent potential to mask off or hide your whole being and your fuller experience from being revealed. The label can become an idea of who or what you are, and what it's like to be you, based on preconceptions around the label rather than the real or true you. Labels therefore have the potential to cover up feelings, what life is like for you, your history and memories, and ultimately block off developing a thorough understanding of yourself and what is true for you.

That is not to say labels should not be used in therapy, but they are a starting point for exploration, a possible means to an end, not an end itself. The label should serve you, not the other way around. Just like you cannot judge a book by its cover, the labelling of you and your emotions can, if not checked, communicate misjudgements about you as well as others. Becoming aware of how you use labels can be useful in your process. Look below the label to what the label means and explore it further.

In addition, the label can, if left unchecked, end up becoming a *self-fulfilling prophecy*. For example, if you believe you will never be a swimmer, then it's unlikely you'll try to find out. It is self-fulfilling because you have labelled yourself when in fact it may or may not be true. Even though your feelings are your personal truth, it is not always an objective one, so it narrows down possibilities. Similarly, if you believe "no one likes you," you may develop an anxiety of fear of people, you're reluctant to make the effort to engage and keep a distance which in turn keeps you away from meeting new people. Subsequently, it reinforces the "no one likes you" label.

Keyword: Self-fulfilling prophecy is any held belief that causes, either directly or indirectly, that belief to become true.

Labels may also be a way of hiding what you truly feel about yourself, and instead you find a preferred way (persona) of presenting yourself. For example, you may say, "I am not scared of anything," as you believe that showing your fears would make you a weak person. In actuality, you may be fearless in certain areas but scared in others, and it's what you feel scared about that may be what is relevant to therapy.

Some people may have or want a diagnosis. Examples of labels include autism, bipolar disorder or post-traumatic stress disorder. In therapy, the diagnosis can help the therapist gain an initial understanding and even inform the way they provide therapy, but therapy sees that very much as a starting point and seeks to look behind the label to the whole person because therapy is more about understanding the whole of you – the inner you, your story, feelings, what has shaped you and how that relates to any problems you share. In therapy, the therapist will be recognising you as more than any label or symptom; they will see you as a whole, unique and complex being.

Another type of label is a brief description; these tell you something of an event, experience or feeling in the client's inner world, but they are still labels because they do not go any further or deeper. Like the synopsis or "blurb" of a book gives you an idea of what the book is about, it does not tell you everything you need to experience to understand it deeply – to do that would require thorough, attentive, absorbed reading and feeling the words expressed by the book.

A *descriptive label* may just be stated in therapy without any follow-up. It misses a lot out.

There is a lot missing in the description; that is why it's like a label too.

"I had an argument last night with my partner, I told him he didn't care and was just using me.. But it didn't work and he just said I need to keep space from him now. I think it is over and I've got to accept it, that's that."

This is a label of an experience that does not go further. For example, what was the argument about? What didn't work? Why is it over? What's your feeling? Therapists are trying to connect with the client's inner world. The labelling occurs here because there is no broader and deeper elaboration that tries to understand the circumstances of what happened and their feelings.

That is not to say that a mental health diagnosis and labelling is bad or wrong when it comes to defining the emotional state or experience you're in. It is more of a concern when it hides you, your true feelings, emotions, thoughts, and experiences. You are more than a label.

Reasons for using labels

How do you use labels? It may be something to explore further in therapy?

- Because it is easier
- As a starting point and to share initial information
- The labels are what people told you. Do you believe others labels of you?
- The labels block the desire to understand further. Labels can be detrimental if it blocks self-understanding.
- It keeps you safe from difficult feelings. Are labels a way of feelings safe from exploring more difficult feelings?

- You prefer the label
- Your ashamed of part of you, so the label is a relief
- A label makes you feel it's not you; rather, it's something outside your control

Spot the labels

Notice the labels in these quotes:

"I'm just too **needy** for my own good. My husband gets annoyed with me when I get needy. I'm worried he will leave me. I'm just going to stop it now."

"I've spent too long in therapy; I'm a **failure.**"

"I'm just **angry** all the time; every time someone tries to dominate me, I try and destroy them."

"I read online about **avoidant personality disorders**. I definitely think that's me."

"I keep pushing people away because I am too **needy.**"

Examples of labels:

➢ Shy/quiet
➢ Needy
➢ Jealous
➢ Angry
➢ Introverted
➢ Bossy
➢ Good, bad or fine
➢ Not normal

➢ Nag
➢ High-maintenance
➢ Crazy
➢ Right or wrong
➢ Attention seeker
➢ An official diagnosis
➢ An unofficial self-diagnosis
➢ I'm fine

Self-Reflection

1. What labels would you use on yourself, in life, in therapy or to label your emotional world?
2. What labels do you like or don't like?
   a. Do you notice any "that's that" type of statements? For example, "I'm ADHD, that's all there is to it."
3. Do you understand where your label came from?
4. Are your labels useful? Why?
5. Do you want to explore more of who you are under the labels? Why?

Am I normal?

One of the most common statements made in therapy, particularly early on in therapy, is whether what you're experiencing is normal. It may be in the form, "Is this is normal," "It can't be normal," or "Am I normal? I don't know." The question is understandable and thus "normal" to ask, because you would like reassurance that you're okay and can be helped. If you're suffering with particular distressing symptoms, like health anxiety, phobias, or OCD, you may find it helpful to know you are not alone and you can get the most appropriate support. A therapist is likely to know about types of symptoms others have experienced and at least be familiar with diagnostic mental health categories.

However, the question that comes to the lips of many therapists is, "What IS normal?" or "What does normal mean?" In other words, what is behind the question you are asking? This is particularly true when clients ask what is normal in relation to their feelings, thoughts and behaviours. Here are some examples of questions from people asking about normality based on emotional states:

"I lost my mother six weeks ago, but I'm crying all the time. This isn't normal, is it? I hate the fact that I can't control it. It's been six weeks. I shouldn't feel like crying all the time."

"My wife and I keep arguing. That happens though, doesn't it? It's normal, isn't it?"

"I keep thinking I just want to run away and escape from my family, including my kids. Surely, that can't be normal?"

"I don't know if I'm doing therapy right. What do other people do in my situation? What's the norm?"

Asking why you feel the need to be in the "normal" category could lead to understanding yourself better. Are you asking because deep down you experience people being critical of you for not being normal? Maybe that's how you experienced growing up at home and you are fearful of standing out or being seen as the "the crazy one," "mad one," or "attention seeker." In turn, perhaps that would ostracise you from your friends, family or cultural system, which you would feel shame for.

Usually, when people ask about normal, they are wanting to be "normal," but it can be that people also don't want to be normal. Having things that set you apart may be a way to feel better about yourself and cope, whether its cuts on arms, personal taste in music, or even a particular mental health label. The desire for individuality and specialness can be found by not following the crowd. Then you have to ask whether you desire to be that way. Is it a way of covering your wounds?

Trying to heal based on trying to fit into a norm is like trying to fit into a mould, and this can cover up how you truly feel and who you "authentically" are. It is not to say you're not part of a bigger society, community, family or cultural heritage, but you are willing to explore your own subjective self-truth. The need to "fit" into a norm could shut off further exploration into you and into what is going on deeper down. For example, you may find the question points to whether you would belong, be accepted, or be loved if you were not normal or as you would like to be.

Self-Reflection

1. Is being normal important to you? In what way? (Think emotionally, as well as externally, such as in a job.)
2. Is not being normal important to you? In what way?
3. Write down ways in which you wish you could be normal during your childhood?
4. Write down ways in which you wish you could be normal as an adult and now.
5. What are your feelings behind the wish to be normal or even not normal? For example, is it to fit in or to know you are healthy?

But I had a good childhood

When you reflect upon your childhood, especially your caregivers and family, it may appear to you that any problems you have now are in no way related. This can be especially true if you did indeed have a good childhood. However, there are a number of perspectives you may wish to consider when deciding whether to bring your childhood into focus within therapy.

Regardless of the way you grew up, the environment, your family, or lack of family, would've had an influence on you, whether it's your beliefs, values or how you experience relationships. I am sure we can all think of something, such as a good teacher who encouraged you to pursue your career or being anxious speaking in front of the school. So, therapy can give you the opportunity to understand how your childhood impacted you and whether it's relevant to your problems. This awareness has the potential to open doors inside you that can guide and deepen your therapy.

Here are a couple of examples when talking about having a *good childhood* was found useful:

Charlie was only 4 years old. He was regularly dropped off to his grandma's house every Tuesday and really enjoyed his time. However, on one occasion, his grandmother was not available, so his father took him to stay for the day at Mike's house. Charlie got on pretty well with Mike and had no issues with staying with him, although it was an unfamiliar environment. As Charlie's dad left him, he said, "Now, you be good boy and have fun but now I have to go." In that moment, Charlie froze and was confused and assumed his dad meant that he may never come back. He was quiet and withdrawn for a while but enjoyed the rest of the day. The fear he experienced was not due to any poor parenting, but now as an adult, he felt those same fearful feelings when he was separated from his partner for long periods of time.

Shirley was an only child and brought up by loving, caring and supportive parents. She could not really wish for more in her childhood and looked back at her childhood as the "best time of her life." She really loved her parents and felt really close to them. However, what she struggled with in adulthood was her confidence and fears of making decisions in her life. She was able to link these problems with her childhood, particularly as her parents would make most decisions for her and tell her what she needed to do. But now she constantly needed their approval to make decisions whether in relationships or when buying some trainers. She said her parents had somewhat "wrapped her up in cotton wool" contributing to her feeling of being unable to face decisions or take personal responsibility for them.

Another common theme in therapy is where you feel conflicted about whether you should talk about your caregivers. The conflict may be because there is a part of you that wishes to talk about your childhood, but another part of you has an overwhelming feeling of guilt, anxiety or even fear about talking about your caregivers in a "negative" way. It just feels judgemental, critical and disloyal. After all, it's not their fault and you're an adult responsible for your problems, aren't you? You don't want to play the "victim" by blaming others for your issues. You have an instinctive protectiveness for them given the importance of the relationship and how you've been supported by them you all your life. Here is an example of this type of conflict where a client is right on the edge of exploring their feelings about caregivers:

"I really don't want to talk about my feelings; it's difficult and I don't want to blame them. I do think my past is related to the way I try to control my emotions and my health anxiety, but I'm worried what happen if I do. I'm scared my relationship will change if I go there."

One way of gently working with your conflicts and anxious feelings is to simply talk about them in therapy and see where it leads you. Exploring feelings about feelings, or meta-feelings, may naturally lead you to the answer of "what to do" and help you to decide whether you want or are ready to explore your childhood further. Sometimes, just by talking about your worries, and their reasons, such as fearing the consequences of disclosure, can lead to more exploration in other areas, and create more safety and a stronger relationship with your therapist.

Exploring your childhood can be about understanding how your caregivers impacted you in life, rather than blaming them, absolving your responsibility, or painting them in a bad light. Looking at your childhood is more about understanding the circumstances of your childhood and whether that can be useful to your healing process. Of course you may blame them, but therapy is about what you feel regardless.

Possible reasons for not wanting to talk about childhood

Remember, these reasons should be seen as valid reasons rather than wrong; it is about whether you wish to challenge them or not.

- You had a good childhood
- Painful experiences
- Unknown consequences of disclosure
- Cannot see how it's relevant to your situation now
- You've got so much other stuff to explore, it's simply not a priority
- You don't wish to be disloyal, critical or blame them
- You wish to take responsibility for your life now
- You wish to keep the image of who your caregivers are in tact

- Feelings of shame
- Wanting to distance yourself from the younger you and the past

Self-Reflection

After you have read this section, reflect on how you feel about your childhood.

1. How would you describe your childhood?
2. What are your best memories?
3. What are your worst memories?
4. Who did you feel closest to?
5. Who hurt you the most?
6. How has it shaped who you are today?
7. Do you believe your childhood is related to your current problems?
8. Are you ready to talk about your childhood more? Why?
9. Do you have any conflicts about talking about caregivers or childhood? What are they?

Summary

- Childhood experiences do influence how we develop into adulthood
- Childhood experiences, even good ones, may be relevant to self-awareness and your problems
- It's not uncommon to find it difficult to talk about childhood. For example, because of guilt or feelings that you're blaming caregivers
- Your conflicting feelings about whether to talk about childhood may in itself be useful
- Talking about childhood is about understanding how your childhood affected you and how it relates to your problems or goals

As always, you decide what feels right for you.

You don't want to change

If your friend complains that he keeps getting into unhealthy relationships, and you respond by saying, "I know you want to change, but you don't really want to," you're likely to be met with a lukewarm response to say the least. However, often when you want to change, it is easy to be so focused on changing that you disregard what you could be losing, in terms of both your identity and your current benefits. For example, if your friend were to explore his relationship style he might find change is difficult for a number of reasons: Perhaps the familiarity of unhealthy relationships, he doesn't don't want to be alone, and the excitement these relationships can generate.

In therapy, you may have a clear sight of what needs to change, or you may discover it as the process unfolds, but even if you are in the darkest of positions, you can usually find something that could keep you from changing if you look hard enough. This is most starkly demonstrated when people in captivity who are abused or maltreated can, even after becoming free, find the change very difficult. They may have sympathy for their abusers, or even a need to be in their captive environment, regardless of the perceived benefits of leaving (changing) their situation. Their transition from captivity to being free is painful.

Here, are some examples of how the desirable benefits of no change can interfere with, or even completely block, change:

- If you give up on an unhealthy relationship, you'll be alone and won't have the good parts of the relationship.
- If you want a healthy lifestyle, you'll have to give up on daily desserts.
- If you want a job, you'll have to give up freedom to dictate how you spend the day.
- If you cut all ties to your caregivers because of abuse, there will never be the possibility of having the parents that you long for deep down.

Any change involves loss. The loss can be so vast it can be like demolishing a big part of your identity. With your loss and the difficulty of transitioning to a new version of you can come many feelings, such as fear, sadness, emptiness, or even an "existential nausea" which can be triggered as a result of being responsible for your own life.

A major challenge you and your therapist may face is when the downsides of change remain out of sight, even buried very deep inside you. I really recommend exploring change proactively, especially when the process feels like it is stagnating, so that any blocks are consciously worked upon.

If you do find reason(s) why change may be difficult, or you find that you're inadvertently blocking it, then you can congratulate yourself for finding out. Reasons for not wanting to change are nothing to be ashamed of; you can practice acceptance, and work with it rather than go into conflict with it. From there, change is possible.

Now let's look at the three types of challenge that change can bring: The loss of advantage, the challenge of transition, and the change of identity. You can use these three categories to reflect upon your own circumstances and, if appropriate, explore in therapy.

The gain of no change

Sometimes, an existing problem and its associated symptoms can have significant advantages which are sometimes called *secondary gains,* or even the less helpful term *self-sabotage or resistance*. Advantages could include monetary benefits, having needs met, personal attention, or to avoid situations that you don't like. In all cases, the problem is reinforced because of the secondary gain.

Here are some examples of the advantage of "no change":

Joe was scared of wasps but it was nice that his wife understood his fear, cared for him and sorted it out. He gained personal attention.

Samuel had a historical difficulty with eating food, but he also hated going to school. He knew he could avoid the worst teachers by blaming it on food issues and lack of energy. If he got better, how would he able to excuse himself?

Narinder was afraid to get close to people. He had always done things on his own and had the persona of being an individual, an outsider, or a rebel. If he dropped his persona of being an outsider, he ran the risk of being hurt by people as well as not feeling special.

Harry was anxious about socialising; he vowed he would do it only once he lost 12 pounds. If socialising is a fear, then the incentive to lose weight diminishes. Unknown to Harry this contributed to him not losing weight.

Margaret feels her husband won't leave her side if she continues to feel depressed or suicidal. Margaret gets her emotional needs met.

Jack gets a lot of care in therapy; if he gets better, he won't be able to get the care he wants.

The pain of change

Change may require you to face the difficulties that will be presented during the therapeutic process, which include making life decisions, facing truths, facing fearful situations, saying good bye, or experiencing emotions.

Here are some examples:

If I start public speaking and get it wrong, I'll feel ashamed and may not be able to do it. The risk of feeling shame is the pain of change.

If I go to therapy, I won't be able to hide (suppress) my thoughts and feelings any longer. I'll have to face my truth. The pain is to own the truth.

I may get myself and my family into trouble if I talk about my brother abusing me. The pain is the risk of disclosure.

If I leave my partner I will have to feel enormous guilt during the process. The pain is the guilt.

So not only look at what you lose but also the challenges and obstacles that lie in your path towards making the change. By airing these challenges in therapy they can be explored further.

The loss of you
Change can also include losing parts of your identity. It can mean saying goodbye to the parts of you that hurt or that are angry, or it may be loss of beliefs which meant so much to you.

An example, the loss of identity can be experienced by some caregivers when their child leaves home for the first time. Not only do they experience the pain of being apart from a loved one, it can also be a big change in their identity. The caregiver is faced with the loss of their role, that of being a constant in their child's life, as well as the loneliness that comes from the change. Needless to say, not all caregivers experience the separation in this way.

Here are some examples of identity or role changes that may be faced during therapeutic change:

I know who I am now. If I change, who am I going to be? And what am I going to do? I am freaked out by it.

I was so angry and hurt by my uncle and how he treated my mum. Now that I've let go of that anger, I feel empty and don't have a purpose.

I have wasted so many years caring for others, but I never paid myself much attention. I feel so sad that I've wasted so much precious time. I don't know what I'll do now.

Who will I be if I'm not alone anymore?

I did so much for myself to get to where I am. Now that I am letting people in, it feels good but also like I've lost a friend inside—a friend I could count on even when I was lonely.

I get into a rage when my partner disappears and goes out with his friends. If I went out with friends too, I would have to accept that we are two separate people, not just "one." It would feel sad and scary.

One way of looking at this kind of loss is to understand that the old parts are still a part of you; you can revisit those parts anytime, without the intensity of their hurt; they become scars rather than wounds. But regardless, the loss of the old parts of "you" may also need to be grieved for in the process of change.

In this way I have explained how the gains of no change can hold back your change process. By giving yourself space to discover and explore these dynamics in therapy you can gain a fuller picture of the things that stand in the way of your change, and what you may want to work on. By understanding the full picture, you can then answer, "Are you sure you want change?" Whether the answer is "yes but" or "no" you can work on accepting it, and that in itself can be the beginning of change.

Self-Reflection

1. Think historically about things you have had to change in your life. Identity things you have been able to overcome versus those you were unable to.
2. Why do you think you were able to overcome or not overcome those "change" challenges?
3. Identify what you would lose, fear, or benefit from by not changing in therapy.
4. Do you believe those things may make change difficult?
5. Is it worth exploring further in therapy?
6. Consider whether you still want change. Why?
7. Reflect on how you wish to work on those change obstacles in therapy or on your own.

It's not their fault

At some point in the process, you will probably talk about or figure out how someone from the past you knew or still know has contributed to your suffering. They will have impacted you and have set in motion a chain of events in your personal history that are related to, even if indirectly, why you're in therapy. This may be as a result of domestic abuse, being adopted, abandoned, neglected, been overly protected or a crime.

Talking about people who have created suffering related to you problems will naturally be part of the process. How can you not talk about your partner when you're thinking of divorce? Or you have been a victim of a crime? When it is someone you don't know it can be easier because there is no conflict in your mind about sharing and understanding your experience and impact they have had on you.

However, in general, as humans are "care" based, talking about people closer in relation to you can be much more difficult, especially when there are many sides to them that are "good." When someone comes into your spotlight that you have or had some form of relationship with, it may inadvertently shut off the possibility of further exploration because "they are not to blame," "they didn't mean to," "it's not their fault" or "even though they hurt me there were good times." This may be due to a sense of fairness, guilt or disloyalty that you are speaking ill of someone.

Exploring people and situations that contributed to your suffering can be more about understanding how they impacted you in life, the circumstances, rather than necessarily blaming them. Of course it does not mean that your relationship with them may not change as a result of the exploration or that you may even end up blaming them. In the end you have the choice to determine whether that can be useful to your healing process or not, you are free to choose.

Self-Reflection

1. Do you have difficulty talking about people who have caused you to suffer? Or have impacted you problems? Why?
2. Do you think it may or does relate to your problems or goals?
3. What would happen if you shared these feelings?
4. If you are conflicted about sharing do you want to talk about the conflict with your therapist?

Why don't others change

Whatever problems you bring to therapy, no matter what path you take, roads you cross or decisions you make, you'll always find that to the largest degree, you'll invariably come back to you. The examination and change of the self is the heart of change. There are three reasons why this is a common factor in the therapeutic success.

First, the obvious fact is that because you want change, only you can change. It is your mind, it is your life and you will only change if something makes sense for you to do so. Regardless of the many talents of a good therapist, they cannot reprogram your mind for you nor would that be ethically right to do so. By spending time in your own mind, sometimes called internal frame of reference, therapy enables you to untangle, restructure and change you. You do it, you really do.

Second, everything in your life is in "relationship" to you. If you're hoping external things like money, career or relationships will alleviate or fix your problems, invariably, they won't, not in themselves. This is particularly true when there are deeper entrenched problems. Because you can't always control external situations, it's the way you relate to external factors in life that usually lead to deeper change, as well as increased resilience to suffering. You changing has primacy rather than relying on others or your external situation necessarily changing.

One way to look to change yourself in your relationships is to continually relate you're suffering back to you, the "I." For example, "my friend went behind my back and bad mouthed me to others" can be related back to the "I" by adding, "this made me [I] feel hurt and humiliated." By sticking with and relating to the "I," there is possibility of your relationship with events and suffering changing over time. By sticking with the "I", you have more chance of experiencing inner change.

Third, sometimes deeper contact with the core hurt inside you is required, and only you can do it with the aid of a good enough therapist. The sad tragedy of a lot of serious psychological problems is that not only do problems in many cases originate outside your control, but you're also left with the hard work of healing sometimes deep inner wounds over many years. In many cases, you will be faced with lines of defence inside you, and it's only with the aid of a good enough therapist that you can "pass defence" and encounter the core hurt within.

Keyword: Defence mechanisms (or as I prefer Protective layers) can be seen as ways of coping, of deflecting from anxious or difficult feelings that are embedded in the mind and body. For example, extreme anger may through work be seen as a defence against feeling the pain of being wrong, inferior or less powerful. " Defence is usually a mechanism, particularly in insight oriented analytic psychotherapy definition, of

protecting and surviving in the world. In many cases defences can remain because of
life experiences even if they no longer serve you best in the here and now.

If you want to break a cycle of self-suffering, because you're looping around the same theme and cannot make external things change, the only choice they have is to change something in you (of course you have a choice not to change as well).

I got a call from my son the other day. They said whether I wanted to come around and see my granddaughter. I just think "beggars belief" how can he ask that, doesn't he know what I am going through. He thinks I'm just making excuses for not coming. He thinks I'm just angry all the time, but I'm the one who has to deal with their father. Where were they?

In this example, it is hoped that the client would do all she could to have a better relationship with her son, but what if she cannot get her needs met? How does she alleviate her suffering, if at all? Through therapy she may not need to understand her feelings more, change her behaviours, grieve over her relationship or accept the situation more.

Self-Reflection

1. Do you use therapy mainly to vent about your situation e.g. relationships issues?
2. Are you relying on your external situation to change to feel better? For example, someone else to change, or a pay rise.
3. Do you reflect on how you can change and be less dependent on external things changing for you?

Note: this does not mean we don't want better relationships or situations in life, it means that we focus on what we can control or influence not what we can't.

I'm wrong

You may already be familiar with the sandwich approach to giving feedback. You begin with what went well, what you may wish to work on more and what you did well again. Coming from anyone in the true spirit of learning and with the purpose of teaching and helping, critique is one of humankind's greatest achievements and it is needed for any form of development. How is it possible to make progress in our learning if it does not contain a critique? Here, the critique is termed feedback, and it is an important part of making judgements necessary to improve the self, others, relationships, work or any learning. Criticism offered in the true spirit of learning is a gift.

However, when it comes to criticising ourselves, we can be the harshest of all critics.

Consider the following examples:

- "I should have done better at school."
- "Why was I so scared? Why didn't I just defend my friend from being attacked?"
- "Arghh, I hate myself for being so fat. I just can't seem to stop eating!"
- "I don't know what to do here. I've been doing therapy for so long, I just feel like a failure."
- "I'm so boring; everyone seems to have such interesting things to say. I can't stand myself."
- "I am disgusting. I hate what I see in the mirror. I hate when my partner even touches me."

In these examples, criticism takes on a different form; rather than being supportive to improve, it is very harsh and punishing. The problem with these types of criticisms is they are shaming, demotivating, anxiety provoking and can be downright scary. The effect of being on the receiving end of these messages could be extremely damaging to how you feel about yourself. The longer-term impact of harsh criticism could include avoiding any situations that trigger these thoughts, and instead of dealing with the problem, you keep busy, procrastinate or even turn to unhealthy addictions. So for example, someone who criticises themselves as boring may avoid social situations and turn to constantly working long hours to avoid feeling.

These criticisms may also impact how we view ourselves overall, that somehow we are defective, weak or bad. When we feel shame we withdraw and disconnect from people as well as ourselves, by finding unhelpful comfort in things like food or drugs, we may mistakenly believe that this will take away the shame and it does but for a short while.

In therapy, you can see this as applying a "hammer to your head." Ultimately what you need to do is find a way of working on ourselves by calming these criticisms and thereby your take care of yourself. So, if you can become aware of an unhealthy critical voice within, you can explore it further during therapy. Notice your self-criticisms and process them "down and out." Having an objective learning mind rather than harsh critical one ultimately is going to give you space to learn and learning involves making mistakes to improve too.

Possible Reasons for the harsh critic

- Introjected messages from experiences of caregivers and people around us. That is, you have taken on board others' views of you and swallowed it as your truth.
- Perfectionism, idealism or very demanding expectations.
- Highly focused on comparison with others.
- Being bullied.
- Linked to how you judge and feel about yourself.

Possible ways to calm the critic:

Usually, the more ingrained and aggressive the criticism, the more therapeutic work is required. Here are some starting points:

- Just be aware and notice it. Say, "Ah, I noticed it."
- Be vulnerable and journal the reasons why, or talk to someone safe about why you feel critical about something.
- Next time you get something wrong, see if you can be more relaxed about not getting it right.
- Use the feedback approach on yourself – what did you do good, what could you improve and what did you do well again?
- Label the inner critic metaphorically, with humour or visually. For example, it could be a big plastic hammer hitting your head or even an obnoxious parody of a colleague criticising you.

Self-Reflection

1. What self-criticisms do you tell yourself? You could also ask someone what they think you do that is detrimentally self-critical.
2. What would you say if someone said those things to a loved partner, friend or child? What do you think the effect of that criticism would be longer-term?
3. What do you feel when you hear those criticisms?
4. What issues does the criticism cause? Does it cause an avoidance of feelings and situations? What behaviours does it influence? For example, not wanting to do things you want.

5. What do you really need to take good care of yourself? Or, what is it that you really need to hear? Express this to your inner critic with feedback.
6. Talk to your critic or write it down as a dialogue as if it were a different person and see what conversation you could have with that part. See if you can gently give that part feedback. You certainly don't want to give the critical part harsh treatment (two wrongs don't make a right!).

Don't be

You can see yourself or individual parts of you in two different ways: the real-self (or authentic true self) is who you truly are, and an ideal-self is who feel you "should" be. The ideal can present as a goal such as getting a promotion, losing weight, or it can present as an internal ideal, such as being serene and not losing your temper. Having an ideal-self is a natural form of forwarding yourself in life, based on desires and goals.

However, because of life experiences, outside pressures, and the need for social acceptance, you can forget the real-self in favour of an ideal self because parts of your real-self become unacceptable or shameful. You feel there is a fundamental flaw in the real-self because you feel strongly that you "should be" living up to the ideal, even though it may be unrealistic, impossible or just not you.

Here are a few examples that signify the partial loss of the real self in favour of an illusionary ideal self. In this first example, the ideal almost takes over the true self:

Sabine grew up feeling weak. She was bullied throughout school life, her studies were affected and she did not fit in to any group. During adolescence, she would often fantasise about being someone else, perhaps a traveller around the world, part of the "cool" group, or a great artist. None of those things were true in reality. But in her mind, and in the world, she presented "as-if," she actually was some of those things. She would continue to be false to people even as she got older. She would pretend that she had a "glamorous" lifestyle and hobbies. This was all an act, even though it still felt real. She could hide her real self not only from others but from herself too.

Sabine believed her true self to be deficient and unlovable, just as others had treated her. The ideal becomes the person she felt she "should" be rather than was. There is a clear distancing of her true self, perhaps based on feelings of self-loathing, where the true parts of her are exiled into a place that cannot be found; banished as being too shameful. Her life learnings and social conditions gave birth to the ideal-self to protect her from being an outsider who did not belong. The false-self became so embedded in her personality that it carried on into her adulthood, making the true parts of her harder to reach. The issue here is that she had lost herself in favour of an ideal.

In the following example, Harry pushes away his real-self in favour for being liked and not having to take responsibility for his own life:

Harry had grown up in an environment where he was never trusted to make his own decisions. He was not allowed to perform activities or take part in new experiences because he was deemed too "fragile and weak" by his caregivers. He learnt to feel not safe enough to learn from his own mistakes. He compensated for this by always trying to fit in by being a "good boy" for his parents. He may not have been good at things his peers were, but he was good at being good.

Now, as an adult, he was afraid of saying what he felt, giving opinions and making a decision. Whenever he had to make a decision he would call his dad in case he got it wrong. When meeting people, he always put on a big smile; after all, "no one likes someone who is miserable," he said. Harry believed that he needed to put on the fake smile in order to fit in and be accepted. He had learnt to be "good" while growing up and letting everyone else do the talking, and so he would not be put in the "spotlight" of life. His true self was largely hidden from the world; no one knew how low and sometimes angry he felt in secret. All this led to him feeling helpless, frozen and unable to make the simplest of decisions. He had learned not to trust himself and therefore was not in a position to take responsibility for his life. All this pretending was just so exhausting.

In the following example, Max had set his ideal so high that he "should not" fail:

Max's ideal self-image was based around being academically excellent. He worked hard, attending classes and completing work on time; most of the time he was used to being top of the class. Max felt good because he lived up to his ideal. However, when his studies begun to suffer after a road traffic accident, he felt he was a loser and was letting everyone down. He sank into deep sorrow as he found himself middling, no longer top of the class. The mismatch between his ideal and his truth caused him so much anxiety that he felt he would rather not submit any work and fail, rather than do his personal best. He ended up leaving the course abruptly because he couldn't face being just good enough.

All these examples show how the authentic or true self can be replaced by an ideal self in response to life's situation, which can affect you in psychologically damaging ways. The ideal in these cases completely replaces a gentler version of "I would like to" with a tyrannical "I must, otherwise I am unacceptable." This unacceptability represents a dictator despising the real you for not being the ideal.

You can check out if there are any unrealistic ideals in your language. Phrases like "I should be" or "I ought to be," may, under careful scrutiny, reveal your harsh ideals. Here are some examples of "should" statements which represent ideals that are unrealistic or "tyrannical":

- I should not make mistakes.
- I should not get angry.
- I should not be weak.
- I should always be happy in front of people.

- I should not say anything negative about people.
- I should be a size 8 (size 14 now).
- I should always be good at anything I do.
- I ought to be wealthier by now (in comparison to Elon Musk!).

Demands in this context can feel tyrannical or like a dictator insisting on the "wrongness" of who you are, unless you meet the demands of an ideal. You are the judge and jury, there is no room for manoeuvre to a reasonable ground so the true self is exiled and held for ransom unless the ideal is met.

The true self may need to be uncovered in the therapy room first because change can only truly happen if the true or real self can be revealed, understood and accepted. Living in the reality of your truth, rather than the ideal is at the heart of the therapeutic process. This does not mean the false parts are wholly false—they may be an expression of you or what you would like, but when they dominate, hiding the real you, your feelings and needs, it can be damaging.

Therapy in this case can be seen as a unification process of the whole (sometimes called holism), by revealing yourself, being vulnerable, taking off the masks, finding disconnected parts and examining their meaning. You may find a way to live not based on an ideal or perfection, but by living with the whole of you as you are, in your truth, directing your life from that point, and in doing so finding a path to emotional health.

You are *you* regardless of what your mind may do to protect you from pain by offering up ideals and masks, or by breaking off parts into an unreachable void. There is only one of you and there is only one of me, and no one can be anyone else. Bring together your parts as a whole, heal and recover your authentic self. Bring yourself home.

Self-reflection

1. Look in the mirror. How do you see yourself?
2. Close your eyes, take a few breaths and get in touch with your own perception of your true-self.
   a. What do you think of your body?
   b. What do you like about yourself?
   c. What don't you like about yourself?
3. Do you feel a dislike of any part of yourself? Why? How does it make you feel?
4. Close your eyes, take a few breaths and then let your mind go to an ideal you, in the future.
   a. What does it look like? Get in touch with your own ideal concept.
   b. Think about your inner ideals (e.g. becoming calmer) as well as outer ideals like job, relationships, and career.

      c.   What will you have to do to achieve your ideal? Is your ideal realistic?

5. What do you notice about the true and ideal "you" that you have envisioned?
6. Can you differentiate between "you" and your "ideal"?
7. Does the ideal serve or hinder you? How?
8. Write down any "should" or "ought to" statements you are known to make. Are they realistic or false ideals?
9. How do you judge your true self? For example, is it gentle like comparing yourself to a friend or a child, or does it feel harsh and hard?
10. How do you think your true self and ideal-self have developed and why?
11. What change would you like to make now?

Acceptance is the acknowledgement of reality. It is a *process* of letting go of a belief that anything could be different, whether it's about yourself or about situations— past, present or pending. Acceptance isn't giving up on change or approval of situations, it is a process of working on reducing your suffering in relation to whatever is causing it.

Acceptance is not something that needs to be forced or made a goal of, because acceptance may be a consequence of the natural unfolding process of therapy, which could include areas of non-acceptance. For example, you may have experienced adverse neglect and abuse, and you're not—or may never be—ready. Acceptance should not be seen as a doctrine that you must move towards, bypassing what you really feel and believe. If you don't accept, or aren't ready to turn towards acceptance, you can accept that too.

However, if you believe you're ready to actively work towards acceptance then read on. Here is an example of something you may be familiar with, to demonstrate how non-acceptance could be detrimental. The same principles apply regardless of the severity or forms of suffering described in this way, and regardless of whether they are situational, the result of a loss, or about yourself.

Imagine that you are running late for an important business presentation. Traffic is going at a snail's pace due to roadworks, and the traffic lights are against you. If you get aggressive towards the drivers and the workmen, it isn't going to get you to work faster, it will just get you stressed and upset. However, if you learned to accept the situation, you'd be resolved to working within it, and have more mental space in which to efficiently navigate yourself to work quicker. You accept the situation as being out of your control. By being less stressed you're also in a better position to do the best you can when you arrive for your work meeting, perhaps even making a joke about it when you begin your presentation.

This example demonstrates how any type of non-acceptance can consist of two types of suffering. The primary suffering— in this case, that of being late—and the secondary suffering, that of being stressed and its consequences.

In this way, quite often I use the term *loosen the grip* or *let go of* rather than *acceptance* because the label of acceptance can imply, even though it does not mean it, approval, or forgiveness of actions. Neither acceptance nor forgiveness approves of bad actions. Approval or forgiveness, either of self or others, may be a part of your process, but I do not want to imply that those things are a must for healing either. Another reason for using these terms is to show that acceptance is not binary, you don't either accept or not accept; acceptance can be seen as anywhere between these opposites. There are degrees of acceptance which may vary over time.

So in therapy, if it makes sense, you can apply the idea of "loosening the grip" to anything you cannot control or influence because there is nothing more you can do. "It is what it is" is an oft-quoted phrase which means while you don't approve or think the situation is healthy, you understand that you cannot do anything more because you cannot control or influence the situation any further.

That is not to say loosening the grip is easy: it's a process, and certainly a part of that process will be to sit with the uncomfortable feelings, giving them space and time to be experienced. It's for you to work out based on your unique set of circumstances and beliefs whether acceptance is an appropriate path for you, as well as the degree of acceptance you are willing to afford.

Self-acceptance

At some point in the process, you may start to feel more accepting of yourself as you are, whether it's certain parts of you, your past or the present situation. When you become more self-accepting, you embrace all or parts of you, not just the bits that you or others like, but all parts of you unconditionally and completely. Self-acceptance can include how you feel about your body, a past mistake, parts you feel ashamed of—literally anything that drives your mental representation of who you are.

It does not mean that you don't want further change in yourself—it is not a resignation letter—it means that you recognise your constraints, strengths, weaknesses and even the darker parts of yourself as your truth. The knowledge of any limitations does not interfere with your ability to accept yourself, warts and all. With self-acceptance, you see the reality of yourself, and work with—rather than against—yourself. You develop self-understanding, care, and compassion towards yourself absolutely and unconditionally.

Self-acceptance—just like acceptance in general—should not be mistaken for approval. Approval may go hand-in-hand with attaining self-acceptance, but it's not a necessary condition. You don't approve of errors you have made or things you could have done differently, but rather accept them as being part of you. Acceptance can have a "that's me" or "it's who I am" quality to it; it embraces who and what you are without resorting to self-attack or losing yourself to masks and ideals which are far removed from your authentic self.

When it comes to acceptance of your errors, you see things as a whole, and find an empathic balance between taking your fair share of responsibility and recognising other perspectives, because in reality it's unlikely if you look deeply, that you were either solely or completely responsible for a particular matter. With acceptance you look towards yourself not as right, wrong, good or bad but as shades of grey. By accepting your errors and, if you can, resolving not to make the same mistake again, you set your heart free from shackles that keep you bound.

From a therapeutic perspective, self-acceptance is regarded by many as a cornerstone in the change process, sometimes called the *paradox of change* which states that change can only occur as acceptance begins. Regardless of any theoretical arguments for acceptance, it is clear to see how judging yourself less can lead to less mental pressure and liking yourself more. How you actually get to acceptance is a process, not through any words you say, but a felt response and an internally held belief. It can take many iterations of working on various parts of yourself before you feel deep down that you can accept yourself partially or wholly. And of course, if you can't, or don't want to, you can accept that too!

Acceptance of parts

Acceptance of parts of yourself, is something to work on in order to deliver further self-acceptance. Here is an example of Josephine getting in touch with an authentic part, and beginning the journey of self-acceptance.

Josephine had worked on understanding her need to appear grandiose in front of others and on understanding why it was there, the purpose it served and how it was not an authentic part of her—it was an illusion that kept her from surviving her upbringing because she felt small and without capability. It was not who she really was, even though it did feel like it at times. Instead she turned her attention and feelings towards her authentic self, the girl that "did not belong", who was rejected and felt not good enough.

It hurt a lot for the next few months, but her self-understanding and self-care increased over time. She lay in her bed nurturing her wounds and said "It's okay, I'm here for you now." Rather than that part of her being hidden or rejected, she began the process of accepting it, and in doing so becoming less grandiose.

Another way in which acceptance benefits the journey, is that rejected parts of you, parts you may feel ashamed about, are allowed to come to the fore. You can work on parts that you may keep hidden maybe even from yourself. To work on acceptance and bringing in of parts of you can move your journey on. Acceptance allows for the parts of you that need to be healed and experienced. Acceptance allows you to focus on the feelings, to allow them in and work with them. It does not mean you don't have feelings about it either, you have of them but it combines with compassion and the desire to try to make things different in the future.

Regardless of the path you take towards acceptance, it will involve revealing your true self, and to do that will require effort in the process to remove your distortions of yourself and of the world and understanding your subjective truth. Now you will be ready to thrive knowing who you are and what you need in life. You've understood and separated the fantasy from the reality, the ideal or false parts of you and have revealed to yourself who you are and what you are not, and gained an understanding of yourself of why, who and what you are today.

Reasons acceptance can be difficult

- You're not ready or would feel guilty or bad for accepting
- Caregivers did not communicate a message that you were okay and acceptable regardless of behaviours
- You identify more with your behaviours more than care for your own being
- Your standards of what you "should be" are very high and almost unattainable
- There are toxic emotions tied with the parts you find unacceptable such as guilt, blame and mistakes
- You have grown with harsh criticism as standard
- If you accepted, it would be like giving in or disrespecting someone in the past
- You would have to let go of the hold of non-acceptance has (See "You don't want to change")

Self-Reflection

1. Are there parts of yourself that you accept? Are there parts you don't accept?
2. Why do you feel it is hard to accept some or all parts of you?
3. How did non-acceptance come about? Consider your history, the environment and external pressures.
4. What do you need in order to accept parts of you as you are, rather than adhering to an ideal?
5. What needs to change for you to feel or experience acceptance?

Chapter 4 – Understanding the therapeutic process

If you're going on a significant journey, it is important to know what to expect, even if it is only to expect the unexpected, and to know how to deal with hardships on the way. In this chapter I describe how the process of therapy tends to unfold and what happens as change occurs.

The questions addressed in this chapter are:

- What is the therapeutic process? What sort of attitude should you have towards it?
- What actually changes "under the covers" as you move through the process?
- Are there particular stages that people go through?

What do we mean by the therapeutic process?

The therapeutic process is the mind, heart and body activity you go through over time to overcome your problems. Healing and growth occur during the process as you work on yourself and your mental world, both inside and outside therapy. The consequences of this activity can lead to changes in the way you feel about your situation, and it is that change that fuels your recovery over time.

Processes of change occur in many systems, like converting milk to cheese, sand to glass or a seed to flower. However, as part of that system of change, there may be multiple steps in the process before arriving at the final product. For example, to produce glass, sand has to be prepared for the correct granularity, and then heated to the right temperature. However, the process does not stop there because it needs further ingredients and activity before it becomes glass.

The process of therapy also involves various ingredients, with multiple steps and activities. However, unlike mechanical processes, the human change process cannot be a cookie-cutter approach. You cannot apply one structured process to everyone and expect it to lead to the desired change. Further, as I describe in this book, change can happen across a number of dimensions in parallel, e.g., less confusion, more action, sometimes seemingly in parallel.

So, how is it possible to convey such a fluid process that will be practical and meaningful? After all, everyone is unique, with their own sets of problems and needs. While it is not possible for me to answer definitively the process you will follow, it is possible to identify the general stages by which people tend to move towards psychological wellbeing and growth. By viewing from the bigger picture of experience and theory, I describe the common stages of healing, as well as the common events that trigger movement towards your desired outcome.

As change occurs, a common set of inner changes may be observable as you move towards wellbeing. Examples of mental change processes may include converting foggiensess to clarity, inauthentic self to a more authentic one, anger to understanding, and fear to safety. However, in order for that change to occur, a bridge is needed, i.e. the process. For example, fogginess to clarity is likely to include making available all the facts about a situation and understanding what caused them.

What changes exactly?

One way to understand the process of therapy is to look below the covers of common changes that take place during the therapeutic process as people move towards psychological wellbeing and growth. For example, what types of psychological and physical changes lead a client from feeling low and confused to energised and hopeful?

In this section, I'll highlight the areas where change commonly occurs, acting as a catalyst for moving the process forward. These dimensions of change can be seen as a continuum from one end to the other, for example, from rigidity to fluidity. As clients move towards overcoming their problems, certain dimensions will be moving, often unnoticed, alongside their process.

It does not mean that everything listed here must change for you to get what you need from therapy. Therefore, you should not make these dimensions into therapeutic goals unless it's something you really want to aim for. How you change and what you change inside is something only you can determine.

Awareness

From being unaware and confused you become fully aware of yourself, your reality and why your difficulties make sense. You're aware of your truth. Awareness has primacy in therapy, as all the other dimensions of therapeutic change may involve significant moments of awareness which can lead to insight and thus change.

Safety

From feeling unsafe and untrusting you move to feeling safe. This applies to therapy, the therapist, the process of therapy and ultimately to all other relationships.

Disclosure

From feeling fearful of disclosing deeper feelings, even to yourself, you feel that you can be open to talk about all sorts of feelings that occur within your inner world, such as memories, shame, fantasies, darker feelings or anything you may have previously felt ashamed to say.

Feelings

From feeling numb, disconnected, suppressing or minimising feelings to become in full contact with your true feelings.

Bodily feelings

From feeling heavy, tense and worn down you feel light, joyful and alive. Sometimes, symptoms may be physical, such as anxiety or panic. Quite often when clients begin to feel better the body feels lighter too.

Thoughts

From thoughts that are overly critical of both the self and of others (including obsessions), thoughts become rational, balanced, assertive and protective of the self.

Self-Worth (Self-Judgement)

From feeling unworthy or inferior, to you feeling worthwhile.

Acceptance

From rejecting yourself, your feelings or parts of you, you fully accept yourself, your feelings and your truth. This does not mean you don't want to change things further but feel accepting of it in the moment.

Moving forward

From being caught up and unable to let go of difficult events and experiences, you go to being able to let go and move forward dynamically, all the while still recognising past significance. Being "caught up" can feel like being trapped in a net and unable to find a way out.

Holism

From having many conflicting, confusing, fragmented or disowned parts you feel resolved, complete and whole.

Separation and Boundaries

You are totally enmeshed in other people's worlds, where you lose yourself and you lose who you are. At the other end of the continuum, you see yourself both as an individual and in relationships with others. You have your own individual needs, thoughts and feelings. You know where you start and others begin.

Identity

From having no identity or misplaced identity you have a genuine connection with an identity. Identity relates to a sense of being and belonging in the world as part of something other than being individual. This may be a culture, spirituality, history, heritage, aesthetic, family, ancestry or personal passions, interests and hobbies.

Relationships

From having painful feelings or no feelings when experiencing relationships you have healthy and joyful relationships. This is not only about relationships with others but also with yourself and the therapist.

It is well recognised that improvements in relationships tend to contribute to improvements in psychological wellbeing.

Fluidity
From holding rigid beliefs and judgements about yourself, others and the world, you become fluid, holding many differing perspectives, and being open to your views being challenged. You move away from black-and-white thinking to exploring many parallel possibilities or solutions. Visually, the stone becomes water.

Confidence or Grounding
From feeling small, powerless and submissive you feel confident and grounded with a sense of inner agency. You have an inner strength or belief in yourself that you can engage more confidently in the world. You are happy with yourself, and happy in your own skin.

Action oriented
From being a passive bystander in life you become fully active in making changes outside the therapy room.

Purpose
From feeling no purpose in life you feel life is full of purpose and meaning, which can be seen as "what makes life worthwhile". For some, it is about a social or political cause, for others, it can be spirituality and relationships. Meanings may change over time for all of us, and can come into focus at various times and stages in life.

Responsibility
From taking little responsibility of shaping your life to taking full responsibility of your life, its meaning and direction.

Stages of the therapeutic process
This section presents a framework for understanding where you are in your therapeutic process and the stages you may go through to overcome your problems.

Each stage has an overarching process theme consisting of various feelings, thoughts and attitudes expressed or unconsciously held. For example, someone who is in the "hesitation" stage will not yet believe therapy can help, or they may guard their feelings involuntarily. However, as the client's inner world evolves they will come to recognise those beliefs and feel safe enough to explore them, moving towards a stage where they are more open with their feelings, even if they feel they "should not" have them.

As you read through the stages, reflect on anything significant that comes up for you and notice whether some of the ideas and inner beliefs resonate. Understanding the process may give you an insight into what you can identify within yourself that you want to work on.

Remember this is a framework to stimulate reflection, rather than an absolute path which you will or must follow to achieve your growth or healing aims. It's a blueprint rather than a map. Only you can define your map.

Key points about the stages:

- The stages are generic and indicative rather than specific to any individual.
- Not all aspects described at any stage will be relevant to you.
- Stages you go through are non-linear. You don't have to pass one stage to get to the next.
- The stages may repeat routinely. You may be at separate stages for each theme you are working on. For example, childhood bullying may be on one track and work stress issues on another.
- Expect plenty of overlap between stages.
- The stages you go through will may be iterative depending on the depth, complexity and scope of change you are looking for. There is a big difference between redecorating a room and rebuilding a house.
- If you're working in short-term therapy, you can still experience all these stages, even in a short period of time.
- Only you can determine what is relevant to your process.

The rest of this section delves into each of the stages.

Stigma (Stage 1)

In the first stage of the process, there is a complete wall against showing feelings and thus therapy is simply sought regardless of any psychological issue. A number of internal beliefs will be at play blocking access to therapy, from feeling "It's not something I do", "I don't believe in therapy" and "There is nothing wrong with me" to feelings of shame or fear of the consequences of therapy.

In very rare cases, such clients may enter therapy but only because of outside pressure or due to a level of mental distress. In such cases, the hope of many clients is that therapy is a procedure to obtain a fix rather than a process. For example, people may enter therapy due to a concerned parent or as a mandatory step during a couple's separation. People at this stage are likely to divert attention away from themselves and their feelings and thoughts may be seen in black and white terms e.g. good or bad, right or wrong. While there is always hope, it is very unlikely that a client will move forward in the therapy process unless there is a "light bulb" moment that removes some of these barriers.

Self-Reflection

Here are some of the characteristics of this stage. Did you encounter any of these?

- Cut off from feelings
- Rigid and way based thinking when making judgements
- Fearful of judgement and consequences
- Feelings of shame
- Holding on to inner and outer exterior image of the self (a social mask)
- Therapy is not an option

In this stage, you're totally against entering therapy and cut off from your feelings with regard to your problems. Which of these voices/beliefs apply to you? If any apply, ask whether they are they holding you back. Reflect on these beliefs and how you arrived at them.

- **"That's just not what we do."**
    - o We don't go outside of the family for help
    - o People will judge you and you'll regret it
    - o We have never done that before so were certainly not going to start now
    - o What doesn't kill you makes you stronger
    - o I never talked; it never did me harm
    - o There is nothing wrong with us
    - o These sort of things happen to other people not us
    - o People who enter mental health support are dangerous people
    - o If you're feeling suicidal or anything else it's your fault no one else's
    - o People who have mental health issues aren't normal, but were normal
    - o Talking about Feelings shows weakness
    - o I don't need therapy
    - o I'm better than this
    - o Suck it up and sort yourself out
    - o It's so shameful to disclose the things you've done
    - o Be a strong boy/man or woman
    - o There is nothing wrong with me
    - o Therapy is a waste of time and money
    - o Other people have it worse than me, I'll just be wasting the therapists time
    - o Therapists pretend to care and are just in it for the money
- **"It's so shameful to disclose the things I've done."**
    - o What will people say or think
    - o That'll be on my record
    - o If I talk I will no longer be able to work / drive

- Sharing personal issues outside of the family is shameful
- **"I fear the consequences."**
  - I'll be judged, criticised or told I'm wrong
  - People won't treat me the same if they know
  - Work will discriminate against me if they find out
  - I won't be able to get work
  - It'll be a waste of time
  - The therapist will say I'm to blame and wrong
  - I don't want to know what's wrong
  - I'm afraid what I will find out about myself
  - Things will never be the same once I know what I've got (a label)
  - I've well to hide parts of me from myself, the therapist may see it
  - It'll be scary and painful if I explore my feelings
  - The therapist will see the guilt, shame and wrongness in me
  - You'll get a brain lobotomy, you won't be the same anymore
  - It's not safe you'll get hurt/worse or abused
  - You'll remember things that aren't real
  - I'll lose friends
  - People will pity, avoid or not trust me anymore
  - People will gossip – school, work, friends and my community
  - I'll be rejected by my group
  - People will be scared to be around me

Hesitation (Stage 2)

In the hesitating stage of the process the client enters therapy reluctantly, maybe as a last resort. They may want the therapy but are—consciously or unconsciously—closed off from the therapy process and the therapist, as well as their own feelings. It seems like they are there in the therapy room but stay away from exploring deeper thoughts about themselves, and certainly no feelings are expressed in the room. Where thoughts are expressed, they can feel like being expressed about someone else, as being remote from themselves or as a generalisation. They may also see therapy as similar to going to a doctor, where they tell the therapist what is wrong and the therapist gives them tools that will "cure" their ailment.

Their own ideas about life may be seen in black and white terms and so could be closed off to the idea of the possibility of seeing things differently. While they may be outwardly confident and in control, they may be unconsciously fearful about therapy, the therapist and the expectations upon them. Clients at this stage may be inwardly conflicted between staying or fleeing therapy, so while there is no guarantee a client at this stage will want to continue, they may, with the right therapist, decide to stay in therapy to see where it leads.

Self-Reflection

Here are some of the characteristics of this stage. Did you encounter any of these?

- The reluctant or tentative client
- See therapy not too dissimilar to going to a doctor
- Will talk about the issue in a general way
- Guards feelings
- Confusion about what to say, think or how things work
- Therapy can be a threat to self-image, values or beliefs

Which of these inner voices/beliefs apply to you?

Feelings inside you:

- I don't have the time or energy for this
- What do I do
- Tell me what to say or do
- I'm scared to tell
- I feel numb or empty
- I feel powerless and hopeless
- I've got to be strong and not show feelings
- Why me?
- I'm useless. I'm not good at anything else how am I going to be good at this.
- No one understands me
- I feel weak
- This is bizarre
- I don't trust myself to know what to say
- Get me out of here as fast as possible I've got other important things to do

Feelings towards the therapist

- Why doesn't the therapist talk more
- Why is the therapist so quiet and just stares
- She seem so cold or strict
- I'm small and they are so big
- They are OK but I'm not OK
- Fix me
- This is not going to work
- You don't matter
- You don't care
- You won't understand
- I feel weak

- This isn't going to work
- I've got to be careful what I say
- I've got to be a good client

Minimisation (Stage 3)

At this stage of the process, the client's initial reluctance to engage in therapy begins to diminish. They begin to feel safer when talking and have developed a level of comfort—but not necessarily trust—with therapy, and in the presence of the therapist.

During this part of the process, the client minimises their feelings by talking about day-to-day things that have happened, as well as symptoms, and the issue. When beginning to talk about feelings they are minimised or avoided outside of awareness, for example, they compare themselves to others, or believe they "should not" be indulging in feelings. These voices may be echoes of past ways of coping with difficult feelings—by suppressing them.

They may still see things in black-and-white terms, either "I" or the "other" is to blame. They feel guilty for talking about those who may have hurt their feelings or contributed to their problems.

Minimisation may also be about what they feel about themselves, such as the lack of ability, capability and power potential they have in life. So going to feelings will feel unsafe, because they don't want to show the person behind the "social mask". They may see the therapist as someone who is more important, more knowing or more powerful than them.

Regardless of how minimisation of themselves is present in therapy, at this stage the client is actively working to get to their subjective truth, even if they feel confused, blocked or unaware of their complete life narrative.

Self-Reflection

Here are some of the characteristics of this stage. Did you encounter any of these?

- No one else is to blame but me
- Sense of personal responsibility for others
- Talks about issues, everyday matters rather than feelings
- Any feelings touched upon are blocked or rationalised quickly
- Feels unsafe or cut off from feelings to talk about deeper matters
- Confusion about what is going on within
- Scared to tell or don't know what to tell

Which of these inner voices/beliefs apply to you?

- Disloyalty
    - I feel guilty for talking about myself because I'll be criticising others
    - It's not my parents fault; I owe them everything, after all (not that it must be the parents fault)
    - It's no anyone's fault
- It's my fault, no one else's
- I'm not normal
- I'm wasting the therapist's time
- There are other people who need more help than me
- I can't feel anything
- I just need to talk about the "symptoms"
- I feel bad for being here
- It's not safe to talk about the real me
    - I'll be hurt
    - Don't trust
    - I'll be judged
- It's me. I'm the problem, not others
- I'm confused
- Everyone else is to blame
- I shouldn't be feeling this way

Revelation (Stage 4)

At this stage, clients will be openly reflecting and overcoming barriers to their subjects of discussion in therapy, such as what happened, and how they feel about themselves and their situation. They begin to join the dots in their understanding of themselves and to gain insights into their way of being, and why that contributes to their difficulties. Things that previously may have felt too difficult to disclose are brought into the room, including feelings of shame and how they feel truly and deeply about themselves.

While they express feelings, they still they have not realised in a true, felt sense the enormity of their loss in life and the impact of it in the here and now. They still see themselves as being unacceptable, even if there is no logical reason for it in the present.

The client takes more responsibility for their own process, sets their own agenda and starts to see therapy and the therapist as being valuable. Confusion begins to subside and their reflections become open, fluid and free. The client goes wherever their mind takes them in the therapy room and begins associating past with present, and in doing so becomes more aware of why they feel the way they do, even if they still encounter conflicts and see themselves as fragmented parts rather than a whole. This part of the process can typically be the longest period in therapy.

Self-Reflection

Here are some of the characteristics of this stage. Did you encounter any of these?

- I should or wish I was x
- I am not really acceptable as I am
- I see myself as parts not as a whole (e.g. I avoid certain parts or feel ashamed of them)
- Feelings begin to simmer
- Small Insights or "A-ha" moments
- Start to talk in first person "I feel x"
- Understand how and why
- I feel lighter and less confused

During this stage, you will also begin to hear a more hopeful inner voice that is becoming more self-aware. Do any of these apply to you?

- Not everything is my fault
- A-ha! I'm starting to get it
- There is a reason I'm feeling this way
- That is not me, this is me
- I feel x
- I can do a, b or c rather than stick with d
- I'm less confused
- Sometimes people let me down

Contact (Stage 5)

Here, the client begins to reach a deeper and broader understanding of their issues and begins to express deeper feelings. They become more aware of themselves, whether it's about relationships, their beliefs, needs or feelings. During this process they will contact more of their raw feelings which may even be felt viscerally, or they may be bodily felt rather than simply narrated. They feel the truth of things in their life in a very real way with any suppressed feelings coming to light. Feelings such as anger, frustration, sadness, and emptiness can be felt in the voice as a "live" happening in the room.

Self-Reflection

Here are some of the characteristics of this stage. Did you encounter any of these?

- This really happened to me
- I'm really angry/sad/teary!
- This really hurts bad
- I get why x
- I can really feel my anger, rage, sadness

128

- I feel worn down
- I feel as if I could explode
- You show your "teeth"

You may encounter some of these changes:

- You feel the feelings not just talk about them
- You understand why you're feeling the way you do
- You react to feelings e.g. emotive and angering
- You realise your loss e.g. opportunities, time.
- Felt heartbreak
- Beginning self-care
- Feeling mentally lighter
- More accepting
- Awareness grows
- Feelings and behaviour change outside of the room
- Hope and trust build
- Self-love

Rebuilding (Stage 6)

The client starts to rebuild their life around what they have learnt during the process. They make life changes over time, sometimes small and sometimes big.

They gain a level of acceptance of themselves and what has happened, and generally feel much lighter in their body as well as in their mind. Their judgements, feelings and thoughts about themselves and others are seen in multiple perspectives, rather than binary. They feel they are able to let go of aspects that were holding them back, although feelings can remain raw. They are in a more self-aware state, and this change of attitude can be seen by others.

Their self-structure (identity, beliefs and mental attitudes) begins to change once they accept themselves, their situation and the reasons for experiencing their problems. However, they don't necessarily know who they are or what it means for them going forward, and they are still undecided on what version of themselves they want to be. They feel more hopeful and optimistic about their life.

Self-Reflection

Here are some of the characteristics of this stage. Did you encounter any of these?

- I believe I am really acceptable as I am
- I'm ok
- Phew... I feel lighter
- I know what I need to do

- Excitement, joy and energy
- Acceptance of difficult parts such as anger
- Who am I now?
- I care about myself and have compassion towards myself

Freedom (Stage 7)

At this stage, inner and outer changes are bedded down and are consistently applied. Clients see themselves as not needing to have a fixed way of being, and can accept themselves for who they are. They accept the whole of themselves, including shades of grey, and their darker sides. They have found a new sense of care, energy and passion in life. The individual trusts their own feelings and life is filled with meaning and purpose.

They continually develop themselves further, have no set structure of who they must be, and are free to choose the direction of both their inner world and life. They are "centre stage" in terms of taking responsibility for their direction. There are no fixed limits to the way they shape their inner life, regardless of external constraints.

They become their own therapists, free to evolve in any way they choose to do.

Self-Reflection:
Which of these feelings / beliefs apply to you?

- Permanent change. A significant shift in your personality.
- You trust yourself
- Life feels full of meaning
- Joy and trust in yourself
- Inner freedom to evolve and choose
- Love unbounded
- Belonging to group(s)
- Deeper connection between self, others, society, world and universe

Need some inspiration? Here are some sayings I have come up with for you to reflect upon during your therapeutic journey. If they don't make sense immediately, pause for a while and reflect on them more or move on to another one. Does anything resonate for you, making you want to explore it more in therapy? What has your therapist said that inspired you?

Get in touch if you have any that helped you or if you want to learn a bit more about what is behind them.

- ❖ Coming to your own understanding of you is best
- ❖ You're the expert of you
- ❖ The best way of understanding yourself more is to understand yourself, yourself
- ❖ No one likes to put their hands too near the fire
- ❖ Follow the illogical to find the logical
- ❖ Therapy is truth, your truth
- ❖ The biggest struggle is the struggle within
- ❖ Don't just dip your toes in, just begin swimming
- ❖ Experience therapy
- ❖ If thinking is easy then feel, If feeling is easy then think
- ❖ Deeper the change deeper the struggle
- ❖ Analysis is paralysis
- ❖ Be prepared for the loss
- ❖ Find you and then you find where to begin
- ❖ Make the illogical logical first
- ❖ Just bring yourself into the room
- ❖ Find the child and find you
- ❖ Nothing changes but you
- ❖ I am me and only me, you are you and only you
- ❖ Turn the volume up inside you, by turning the volume down outside
- ❖ Centre Stage, not left, right, above or below
- ❖ Beware false images and concepts

- ❖ You say your feelings are wrong, look for why they are right
- ❖ Leave your toolbox outside the room
- ❖ The therapist is the tool
- ❖ You heal you, you do it
- ❖ I do nothing yet all is done
- ❖ You can only go so far as the therapist has gone themselves
- ❖ Try harder than the therapist

Are you in therapy or are you about to embark on a therapeutic journey? Do you need help? Are you feeling stuck, emotionally overwhelmed, or confused by the healing and growth process of therapy? Do you want to know what direction your healing process should take? Do you need help in figuring out what you need to do to make the process as effective, efficient, and safe as possible? Then these services could be for you.

To support your therapeutic process, I offer the following:

- A secure "Ask the therapist" messaging service
- Online secure coaching (instant messaging, audio, or via web conference)
- YouTube channel "Dear therapist" for each of the ways
- Consumer events (online/offline)

You can find details of each service at empoweringyourtherapy.com.

*These services are for anyone around the world where there are no legal constraints in providing support. It is not for **previous or existing clients for ethical reasons.***

Ask a therapist

If you want to ask me a specific question, you can contact me on the "Ask a therapist" page at empoweringyourtherapy.com.

You can ask questions and they will be answered by a therapist. We will provide some thoughts, reflections, and guidance. The guidance will not be telling you exactly what to do.

Please note that due to legal jurisdiction I may not be able to answer questions if you are based in a particular country.

Online therapy coaching

I also hold confidential online coaching session for clients who need external support for their therapy process. Coaching is based on the principle of working on things that help or hinder you. I do not tell you what to do, but I help to inform your decisions.

The ethics of this services are the same as for psychotherapy and counselling. In particular please note:

- It is confidential unless there is serious harm to yourself or others
- We will provide a safe place for you to share thoughts and feelings from different perspectives and help you to find your own answers
- We will ask questions to help you focus on what's going on but we remain impartial to any decision you make about the direction of your therapy
- We share concerns if something about your process is or maybe harmful to you.

During this process I ask you to fill in a 50 point questionnaire to elicit your feelings and how you are in the room in order to provide some suggested activity to help you with whatever you are struggling with in therapy.

Consumer events

I also hold regular events online and in person for consumers of therapy services. Regular event dates can be found on empoweringyourthearpy.com. Here are the general event details:

This is a psychoeducation event for general public/clients, who are stuck, confused or have overwhelming feelings and emotions that have been created by the therapeutic encounter and process (counselling and/or psychotherapy of any form including individual, couples, group and family therapy).

The types of issues that clients can encounter that could impact their lives include:

- Unsure of direction therapy should take.
- Unsure how to make therapy work for you.
- Don't know whether to stay or leave the therapist.
- How to make therapy efficient, effective and safe.
- Not sure if the therapist is right for you.
- Not sure if you are using the right type of psychotherapy (counselling, CBT, EMDR, DBT etc..) or what options I have.
- Confused feelings towards the therapist.
- Stuck and not making progress.
- Feeling that no therapist is able to help.
- Continuous cycle of starting/ending therapy.
- Finding it hard or ashamed to say things to the therapist you would like to.
- Feeling a loss/attachment towards the therapist even after ending therapy.
- Feeling abandoned by the therapist.
- Feeling angry/frustrated at the therapist.
- Feeling your being blamed by the therapist.
- Feeling the therapist is not being open and/or withholding information.
- Constant thinking about the therapist.
- Emotional and/or therapist abuse, e.g., anger directed towards client.
- Difficult endings in therapy.
- Love and/or sexual attraction.
- Finding it hard to end therapy.
- Detangling feelings between that of a friend and therapist.
- Boundary/ethical issues.

Please note I do not provide a complaints service or a mediation service between the client and therapist or between the client and a professional body.

Contact the author

For questions relating to this book email: ma@paththerapy.co.uk

About the author

Mamood Ahmad is a clinical psychotherapist (UKCP Registered) and educator who originated and developed learning oriented therapy, a form of therapy coaching, which focuses on empowering clients to effect their own change within safe and ethical healing relationships, including counselling and psychotherapy.

Prompted by his own experiences of not knowing what to do in therapy, he provides specialised *therapy coaching* to consumers of therapy who feel stuck, emotionally overwhelmed or confused by therapy. His research interest is client perspectives of therapy and how they inform practice.

He has nearly 10 years of therapeutic experience working in private practice with adults, young people, and couples. He is based in the village of Binfield, Berkshire, UK. He is passionate about wing chun (A Chinese martial art), and philosophy.

Learning oriented coaching focuses on the client's learning process to effect their desired change against their goals, rather than any specific theory of psychological disturbance.

Printed in Great Britain
by Amazon

87539388R00082